MORE FEASTS FROM THE

EAST

Roz Denny

SIMON & SCHUSTER

A VIACOM COMPANY

First published in Great Britain by Simon & Schuster, 1998
A Viacom Company

Simon & Schuster Ltd
West Garden Place
Kendal Street
London W2 2AQ

Design: Moore Lowenhoff
Cover design: Jane Humphrey
Typesetting: Stylize Digital Artwork
Photography: Steve Baxter
Styling: Marian Price
Food preparation: Jane Stevenson

Weight Watchers Publications Manager: Juliet Hudson
Weight Watchers Publications Assistant: Celia Whiston

ISBN 0 68484 020 0

Printed in Hong Kong

Pictured on the front cover: *Sweet and Sour Tiger Prawns (page 23)*

Pictured on the back cover: *Mango Yogurt Mousse* and *Indian, Pawpaw and Pineapple Platter (page 74)*

Recipe notes:
Egg size is medium, unless otherwise stated.
Fruit and vegetables are medium-sized, unless otherwise stated.
It is important to use proper measuring spoons, not cutlery, for spoon measures.
1 tablespoon = 15 ml; 1 teaspoon = 5 ml.
Dried herbs can be substituted for fresh ones, but the flavour may not always
be as good. Halve the fresh-herb quantity stated in the recipe.

Ⓥ shows the recipe is suitable for vegetarians.

Contents

Introduction

The cuisines of the Far East are among the most sophisticated and ancient in the world. The ingredients are cheap and colourful and the techniques simple and fast. In the West we are increasingly influenced by the cooking of China, India and Thailand, not just because these cuisines are so delicious, but also because they are easy to recreate in our kitchens.

Many Eastern dishes may seem exotic but almost all the basic ingredients are easy to find. The sauces, spices, oils and relishes which add an authentic touch are widely available. An increasing number of supermarkets have special ethnic food sections and many corner shops run by storekeepers of ethnic origin stock essential ingredients.

Some of the ingredient lists in this book look alarmingly long. In fact most of them are small amounts of sauces or spices – easily measured and quickly added. They keep well so once you have bought, say, a bottle of oyster sauce or a jar of cardamoms you will find they keep for months.

Here are a few of the most important ingredients in the cuisines of the Far East.

Some Common Ingredients in Asian Cooking

Oils: all of these are high in Points and Calories so use very sparingly. Groundnut oil, coconut cream and ghee are traditional and are generally highly flavoured so a small trickle will often suffice. Sesame oil can be used a teaspoon at a time to add an Oriental flavour. Sunflower oil is a good all-purpose oil when used sparingly.

Soy sauce: made from fermented bean curd and therefore vegetarian. Light soy sauces are the most popular in Chinese cooking and are ideal for fish, chicken and vegetable dishes. Dark soy sauces have a deeper flavour and a darker colour and are more suitable for dark meats and long, slow cooking. Naturally brewed and tamari soy sauces are made in traditional ways and have richer flavours.

Oyster sauce: made from dried oysters and used in the same way as soy sauce. It is possible to buy vegetarian oyster-flavour sauce.

Hoisin sauce: a thick barbecue-style aromatic sauce with a plum-flavoured base. It is used in making Peking duck and Char Sui pork.

Thai fish sauce (Nam Pla): made from dried fish in southern Thailand and used liberally like soy sauce. Use light soy sauce if you can't find it, but it should be easy to find in supermarkets.

Dried shrimps: used in South-East Asian cooking and sold as a paste called terasi or kapi. You only need to use a small amount and it stores well. It is available in Oriental food stores. There isn't really a substitute although anchovy paste is slightly similar.

Rice wine vinegar: much lighter and slightly sweeter than our Western vinegars. It can be used in the same way as ordinary vinegar in dressings. It is available in supermarkets.

Rice wines: an important flavouring in many Japanese dishes. It is made from rice, yeasts and spring water. If you can't find the real thing, then use a pale dry sherry. There are two sorts of Japanese rice wines: sake and mirin. Sake is quite strong. Dry sherry or dry vermouth are acceptable substitutes for either of these.

Coconut: sold as milk or creamed. It is rich and quite fattening. To get a similar flavour, you can steep some desiccated coconut in boiling water and use the drained liquid.

Coriander: the most popular fresh herb in Asian cooking. It is easy to find in supermarkets, however ethnic shops sell large bunches much cheaper. As a substitute you could use flat-leaf parsley but the flavour will not quite be the same.

Lemon grass: looks like a pale salad onion. Fresh lemon grass has a delicious fragrance and is increasingly easy to buy. It keeps for at least two weeks in the fridge. Dried lemon grass and purées don't have as good a flavour so do make an effort to find the fresh sort.

Ginger: pungent and spicy, fresh root ginger is a very popular Asian spice. Although you only need a small amount for each dish, it's a good idea to buy large pieces of root and keep them wrapped in plastic bags in the fridge or freezer since they keep for ages. You could also peel and grate the whole piece, cover it with dry sherry, and then store it in a screw-top jar in the fridge.

Chillies: fresh chillies are sold in a wide variety of sizes and colours. For the most part, large chillies are juicier and milder than the small ones and red ones are more fiery than green ones. Slit the chilli to scrape out the seeds and then slice or chop as required. Chilli juice can sting, so don't rub your eyes with your fingers after handling chillies.

Sichuan peppercorns: red, sweetly aromatic flower buds which add a very distinctive taste. They are available in Oriental shops and larger supermarkets. It is worthwhile buying them when you see them and storing them for future use since they keep indefinitely.

Saffron: the dark orange and red threads have a strong, slightly bitter flavour but a wonderfully pungent and sweet scent. It is used mostly for special occasions because it is expensive. It is especially good in rice dishes such as Indian pilaus. The best way to draw out its flavour is to mix it with a little boiling water or hot stock and then stir into the dish.

Bay leaves: have a distinctive fragrance and can be used in marinades, meat dishes, soups and stocks.

Cardamoms: sold as small green pods and can be used in sweet and savoury dishes. Use the pods whole and then remove them before serving if necessary.

Cinnamon sticks: made of the dried, rolled bark of a tropical evergreen tree native to Sri Lanka, southern India and the West Indies. The sticks are especially good for spicy meat or vegetable dishes. Remove them before serving.

Curry powders: are blends of ground spices available in various strengths. The heat of a curry powder is determined by the amount of chilli pepper or cayenne which is added. A wide assortment of mixes such as korma or tandoori are available.

Garam masala: an intensely aromatic mixture of milder spices such as cumin, coriander, cardamom and black pepper. Unlike curry powder, it is always added near the end of the cooking time and can be sprinkled over meat or fish before grilling.

Dried herbs and spices: should always be used by the 'best before' dates. After these dates, they lose their pungency. Always store spices and dried herbs in a place away from daylight. To release the full aroma of dried spices, it is best to lightly fry them in a little oil, but since this adds Points and Calories, you can either dry-fry them in a small non-stick frying-pan or mix them with a little boiling water.

Asian pastes and purées: most cooks in India, South-East Asia, China and Japan use ready-made spice pastes. These are very useful but be aware that many of them contain oils and fats. Garlic, ginger and chilli are sold as purées in small jars or tubes. These are an acceptable alternative if you can't find the genuine ingredients but many have a pasteurised flavour and therefore don't taste entirely authentic. However if a recipe only needs small amounts of ginger or garlic, purées are quite suitable.

Asian 'dairy' products: the most common are yogurts (for Indian cooking) and soy bean curd, also known as tofu, which is a low-fat, high-protein food. Creamy yogurts are more traditional, but low-fat plain yogurts are excellent for low-calorie dishes. Tofu is sold in blocks which should be drained, patted dry and then cut into cubes. Normally, tofu is fried until golden to develop the flavour, but you can also 'dry-fry' the cubes in a hot non-stick frying-pan until browned or grill the tofu as a whole piece and then cut into cubes. For more flavour, try marinated or smoked tofu. Paneer is an Indian cheese, but it is high in fat so use it sparingly.

Rice and Noodles

Rice is used as a base in almost all Asian meals and is often eaten up to three times a day. In Indian and Chinese cooking long-grain rice is the most common. Short-grain, sticky rice is found in Thai, Japanese, and sometimes in Chinese cooking. Try to buy good quality rice since it will have the best natural flavour. Avoid 'easy-cook' rice which claims to be 'non-stick'; the taste will be very inferior. For best results, I recommend Indian basmati and Thai jasmine rice. Both of these have a lot of natural fragrance. They may cost a little more but it is worth it because you will not be tempted to add butter or oil to make them taste better. When cooking rice, generally allow 50 g (1¾ oz) per person but it's not really worth cooking less than 100 g (3½ oz). If you have any leftovers, don't worry, cooked rice will store well for up to three days if covered and refrigerated.

In China, noodles of all types are eaten both day and night and can be found everywhere: on the family dinner table, in food stalls, in restaurants. They are very nutritious and are usually of good quality. Noodles are made from wheat, rice flour and buckwheat and are sold in all shapes and sizes. Most supermarkets now also stock both the fresh and dried varieties. They are very simple to prepare.

To cook basmati rice: for 2 servings, rinse 100 g (3½ oz) of uncooked rice in a sieve under cold running water for about 1 minute. Bring a large pan of water to the boil. Add 1 teaspoon of salt and stir in the rice. Stir well and return to a medium boil. Cook uncovered for 10 minutes. Drain, rinse in hot running water and leave to stand in the colander for 5 minutes before forking through.

To cook Thai jasmine rice: for 2 servings, put 100 g (3½ oz) Thai rice into a small saucepan with 200 ml (7 fl oz) water. You do not need to rinse the rice before cooking. Thai rice is served unsalted so do not add salt to the water. Bring to the boil, stirring once or twice and then turn down to a gentle simmer. Cover and cook for 10 minutes. Remove from the heat, still covered and leave to stand for 5 minutes before serving. The rice will be slightly sticky.

To cook noodles: follow packet instructions. To serve noodles plain, toss them with ½ teaspoon sesame oil and sprinkle with a good pinch of sesame seeds.

Soups and Starters

Starters are a Western idea, but there are plenty of dishes in the Asian repertoire which you can use to begin a meal. There are lots of light dishes as well as a great tradition of snack-type treats which are bought from street vendors. There are also many kinds of soups, which are generally served at the end of a meal to clear the palette.

Lassi (Indian Yogurt Drink)

Serves: 2

Preparation time: 5 minutes
+ overnight setting
Calories per serving: sweet lassi with mango 120; savoury lassi or sweet lassi without mango 90

Freezing: not recommended

Ⓥ

Popular in many parts of India, lassi is a light, refreshing drink which is perfect for a hot day or with a spicy meal.

500 ml (18 fl oz) skimmed milk
2 tablespoons live yogurt
some chopped fresh mint or two good pinches of dried mint
For a savoury drink:
1 teaspoon sea salt
1/2 teaspoon ground cumin
For a sweet drink:
1 small ripe mango (optional), peeled and flesh removed from the stone
artificial sweetener, to taste

1. Bring the milk to the boil so it just starts to bubble around the sides of the pan and then remove. Allow to cool until tepid.
2. Mix in the yogurt. Pour it into a vacuum flask and allow to stand overnight, or stand the milk in a warm place overnight. An airing cupboard or on top of a boiler will do fine. When the milk is ready, it will have set to light curds.
3. Whisk the milk lightly and flavour as sweet or savoury. For savoury lassi, add salt and cumin to the curds and then thin the lassi down with a little cold milk until it is quite runny. For sweet lassi purée the mango (if using) in a food processor and then add the set curds and sweetener to taste. Finally, add cold water until the lassi is quite runny.
4. Chill the lassi until required and then stir in some chopped fresh mint or sprinkle with a pinch of dried mint.

Points per serving: sweet lassi with mango 2; savoury lassi or sweet lassi without mango 1
Total Points per recipe: 8 or 4

Chicken Noodle Soup with Peas

Serves: 3

Preparation and cooking time: 20 minutes
Calories per serving: 80

Freezing: not recommended

This light and clear Chinese-style soup is filling, yet low on Points and Calories. Ideally, use home-made chicken stock. Otherwise, use a good quality chicken stock cube or try a sachet or two of Japanese miso soup mix.

100 g (3 1/2 oz) egg noodles, broken in pieces
1 teaspoon sesame oil
100 g (3 1/2 oz) skinless, boneless chicken breast, cut into thin, bite-sized strips
1 garlic clove, chopped
1 teaspoon grated fresh root ginger or ginger purée
1 litre (1 3/4 pints) chicken stock or Japanese miso soup mix
2 tablespoons light soy sauce
1 tablespoon dry sherry or dry vermouth
2 salad onions, sliced thinly
1 red chilli, de-seeded and sliced thinly (optional)
50 g (1 3/4 oz) peas
a few sprigs of fresh parsley or coriander (optional)
sea salt and freshly ground black pepper

1. Cover the noodles with boiling water. Leave for 4 minutes and then drain and set aside.
2. Heat a non-stick saucepan and when it is hot add the sesame oil and then the chicken pieces. Stir-fry for 2 minutes with the garlic and ginger.
3. Pour in the stock, soy sauce, and sherry or vermouth. Season well and bring to the boil.
4. Simmer for 5 minutes and then add the salad onions, chilli (if using) and peas. Continue to simmer for a further 5 minutes. Stir in the noodles
5. Check the seasoning and serve immediately with a few sprigs of parsley or coriander (if using).

Points per serving: 3
Total Points per recipe: 9

Sweetcorn and Prawn Soup

Serves: 4

Preparation and cooking time:
20 minutes
Calories per serving: 75

Freezing: not recommended

Sweetcorn is a good source
of fibre.

125 g (4^1/$_2$ oz) peeled prawns,
   thawed if frozen, patted dry
   and chopped roughly
2 tablespoons light soy sauce
1 teaspoon sesame oil
1 leek, sliced thinly
1 small carrot, grated coarsely
   or cut into very thin sticks
1 teaspoon grated fresh root
   ginger or ginger purée
1 litre (1^3/$_4$ pint) chicken, fish
   or vegetable stock (made
   from a cube)
275 g (9^1/$_2$ oz) canned creamed
   sweetcorn
1–2 tablespoons dry sherry
sea salt and freshly ground
   black pepper

1. Sprinkle the prawns with 1 tablespoon of soy sauce and leave for a few minutes to marinate.
2. In a non-stick saucepan, heat the sesame oil and then quickly stir-fry the leek and carrot for about 2 minutes. Add 2 tablespoons of water if the mixture looks a little dry.
3. Add the ginger and then the stock, creamed sweetcorn, remaining soy sauce and sherry. Bring to the boil, simmer for 3 minutes and then add the prawns. Cook for another minute and then check the seasoning. Serve hot.

Points per serving: 1^1/$_2$
Total Points per recipe: 6

Tom Yum Soup

Serves: 4

Preparation and cooking time:
20 minutes
Calories per serving: 80

Freezing: recommended

Tom Yum is a popular spice paste in Thailand which you can make quite easily at home since more and more supermarkets now stock Thai foods. If you can't find Thai fish sauce, use soy sauce with a little anchovy essence. Use any leftover paste in casseroles and stir-fries.

For the Tom Yum paste:
2 tablespoons sunflower or
   groundnut oil
3 garlic cloves, crushed
1 small onion, chopped finely
1 large red chilli, de-seeded and
   chopped finely

3 tablespoons Thai fish sauce,
   or 3 tablespoons light soy
   sauce +1 teaspoon anchovy
   essence
^{1}/$_2$ teaspoon salt
1 teaspoon sugar
For the soup:
1 litre (1^3/$_4$ pints) chicken stock
1 fresh lemon grass stem, sliced
   very thinly
2 dried Thai kaffir lime leaves
   or zest of 1 lime
juice of 1 small lemon
2 salad onions, sliced thinly
100 g (3^1/$_2$ oz) cooked chicken
   breast, pulled into small
   shreds
100 g (3^1/$_2$ oz) button
   mushrooms, sliced thinly
6 baby corns, sliced diagonally
a small handful of fresh
   coriander or flat-leaf parsley
sea salt and freshly ground
   black pepper

1. First make the paste. Heat the oil in a small pan and gently fry the garlic, onion and chilli for 3 minutes.
2. Add the fish sauce or soy sauce and anchovy essence, together with the salt and sugar. Cook for a minute and then place in a food processor to blend to a purée, adding a little water if necessary until smooth. Scoop into a small jar.
3. For the soup, put the stock into a saucepan with the lemon grass, lime leaves or zest, and lemon juice. Add the salad onions and half the Tom Yum paste. Bring to the boil and then add the shredded chicken, mushrooms and baby corns.
4. Turn down to a simmer and cook for about 3 minutes. Add the coriander or parsley sprigs and check the seasoning. Serve hot. Store the remaining paste in the fridge for up to 2 weeks or freeze and use within one month.

Cook's note:
Thai kaffir lime leaves can be found in most supermarkets beside the other packets and jars of dried herbs and spices.

Points per serving: 1
Total Points per recipe: 4

Chicken Satay with Peanut Dipping Sauce

Serves: 4

Preparation and cooking time: 15 minutes + 1 hour marinating
Calories per serving: 125

Freezing: not recommended

Serve on a bed of light salad leaves such as lamb's lettuce, rocket or finely shredded Chinese leaves. Feel free to add any Oriental leaves you can find such as Thai sweet basil; increasingly, super-markets are stocking small packets of intriguing leaves which are fun to try out. You will also need 8 wood satay sticks.

1 fresh lemon grass stem (optional), chopped
2 garlic cloves, crushed
2 pinches of ground white pepper
1 teaspoon ground turmeric
1 teaspoon ground coriander
$1/2$ teaspoon salt
3×100 g ($3^1/_2$ oz) skinless, boneless chicken breasts, cut into bite-sized pieces

For the sauce:
1 tablespoon crunchy peanut butter
150 ml ($1/4$ pint) water
1 garlic clove, crushed
1 teaspoon soy sauce or Thai fish sauce
2 teaspoons dry sherry
1 teaspoon caster sugar
2 teaspoons fresh lemon juice
$1/2$–1 tablespoon sweet chilli sauce

To serve:
a small selection of salad leaves
1 lime, quartered
1 salad onion, cut into thin shreds

1. Mix the lemon grass with the garlic, pepper, spices and salt and then add the chicken. Cover and set aside in the fridge for about an hour to marinate. Soak 8 wooden satay sticks in cold water.
2. Meanwhile, make the sauce. Simply put the peanut butter into a small saucepan with the remaining ingredients and slowly bring to the boil, stirring once or twice. When smooth, set aside until ready to serve.
3. Preheat the grill or non-stick ridged frying-pan. Thread the chicken pieces on to the satay sticks, pushing them down to the pointed end. Grill for about 3 minutes on each side until nicely browned.
4. Reheat the peanut sauce gently and pour into a small bowl. Serve the chicken on a bed of salad leaves with the lime quarters and scatter over the shreds of salad onion.

Points per serving: 3
Total Points per recipe: 12

Stir-fry Vegetables and Noodles in Lettuce Cups

Serves: 4

Preparation and cooking time: 20 minutes
Calories per serving: 260

Freezing: not recommended

Ⓥ

Tofu is a high protein bean curd – the tastiest tofu is smoked or marinated and it can be dry-fried for extra flavour.

1 round crisp lettuce or large radicchio
125 g ($4^1/2$ oz) egg noodles
1 teaspoon sesame oil
2 tablespoons light soy sauce

200 g (7 oz) pack of smoked or marinated tofu
1 tablespoon sunflower oil
1 carrot, cut into long thin sticks or grated coarsely
100 g ($3^1/2$ oz) mange-tout peas, sliced diagonally
15 cm (6 inch) piece of mooli (Chinese white radish), peeled, halved lengthways and sliced thinly
1 garlic clove, crushed
2 teaspoons chopped fresh ginger or ginger purée
2 salad onions, sliced thinly
1 teaspoon sesame seeds, preferably toasted
salt and freshly ground black pepper

1. Remove any limp outside leaves from the lettuce and then carefully peel off four large leaves to make four 'cups'. It doesn't matter if they are slightly torn. Cover and chill.
2. Break the noodles roughly and soak in boiling water according to the pack instructions. Drain and toss with the sesame oil and 1 tablespoon soy sauce. Keep warm.
3. For the stir-fry, cut the tofu into small cubes. Heat half the sunflower oil in a wok and stir-fry the tofu until golden brown and crispy. Remove and add the remaining oil.
4. Stir-fry the carrot, mange-tout peas and mooli for about a minute. Add the garlic, ginger and salad onions and cook for another minute or so. Stir in the remaining soy sauce and toss with the noodles and tofu cubes.
5. Arrange the lettuce cups on a platter. Check the seasoning of the stir-fry and spoon straight into the waiting lettuce cups. Scatter over the sesame seeds and eat promptly!

Points per serving: 3
Total Points per recipe: 12

Sushi

Serves: 4

Preparation and cooking time:
25 minutes
Calories per serving: 135

Freezing: not recommended

Ⓥ

To make sushi at home, you just need some special seaweed called nori and lightly sticky rice. They can both usually be found in large supermarkets with ethnic ranges. A sushi roll mat helps too, but non-stick baking parchment is a good substitute.

100 g (3½ oz) Thai jasmine
  rice or sushi rice
1 tablespoon rice wine vinegar
½ tablespoon caster sugar
½ teaspoon salt
½ cucumber
1 egg
2 teaspoons light soy sauce
1 teaspoon sunflower oil
3 sheets of nori seaweed
freshly ground black pepper
To serve:
Japanese soy sauce, e.g.
  Kikkoman or Tamari
a few shreds of salad onion

1. Put the rice into a saucepan with 250 ml (9 fl oz) water but no seasoning. Bring to the boil, cover, and simmer very gently for 10 minutes. Do not lift the lid.
2. Mix the wine vinegar with the caster sugar and salt as a dressing. Remove the pan from the heat and allow to stand for 5 minutes. Then stir in the rice dressing. Cover again and make the fillings.
3. Cut the cucumber in half lengthways. Remove the seeds and then cut into strips. Trim the strips so that they are as long as the nori sheets are wide.
4. Beat the egg with the light soy sauce and some pepper. Heat the oil in a small non-stick frying-pan and pour in the egg. Cook over a gentle heat so that it resembles a thin pancake-like omelette. Do not stir. To maintain a flat surface, burst any bubbles which pop up. Cover the pan for the last minute or two to let the top set.
5. Tip the omelette on to a board and pat dry with kitchen paper. Trim roughly to a square and then cut into 3 equal lengths. Fold each length in half lengthways.
6. Now make the sushi. Lay a nori sheet on either a sushi roll mat or a large sheet of baking parchment. Spread over a third of the rice but leave a margin of approximately 3 cm (1¼ inches) at the end.
7. Place a folded egg strip in the middle widthways, together with 2 strips of cucumber. Using the sushi mat or baking paper, roll the top of the nori sheet firmly over the rice and fillings like a Swiss roll. When you get to the end, give it a good squeeze, remove the mat and put the roll, join-side down, on a plate.
8. Repeat with the remaining nori, rice and fillings. Cover with clingfilm and chill. Cut each roll into six. Arrange on a dark platter. To serve, put the Japanese soy sauce into a small bowl and scatter with a few wisps of salad onion.

Cook's note:
Seaweed sheets are usually found with oriental ingredients such as soy sauce. The packet usually has a helpful diagram which illustrates how to roll sushi.

Points per serving: 2½
Total Points per recipe: 10

Balti 'Ratatouille' with Poppadums and Yogurt

Serves: 4

Preparation and cooking time:
25 minutes
Calories per serving: 205

Freezing: recommended

(v)

Balti cooking involves quick stir-frying with Indian spices. Traditionally, the food is then served in a karahi, which is shaped like a small wok. It's a way of cooking that works well with aubergines and courgettes and the other ingredients that make up a ratatouille.

1 small onion, sliced
1 yellow or red pepper, de-seeded and sliced thinly
½ small aubergine, diced
2 courgettes, sliced
1 tablespoon sunflower oil
2 garlic cloves, crushed
1 tablespoon finely chopped fresh root ginger or ginger purée
1 fresh green chilli, de-seeded and chopped
1 tablespoon mild or medium curry powder
425 g (15 oz) canned green lentils
sea salt and freshly ground black pepper
To serve:
8 poppadums
150 ml (¼ pint) low-fat plain yogurt
2 tablespoons chopped fresh mint or coriander
½ teaspoon ground cumin

1. Put all the chopped and sliced vegetables into a food bag with the tablespoon of oil and shake well to mix. Heat a non-stick karahi or wok until hot and then tip in the vegetables and stir-fry for about 3 minutes until softened.
2. Add the garlic, ginger and chilli, cook for another minute and then stir in the curry powder and cook for yet another minute. Pour in the lentils with their can liquor, season and bring to the boil. Reduce the heat to a simmer. Cook for about 10 minutes, stirring occasionally, until the vegetables are softened and the liquid is reduced to almost nothing.
3. Meanwhile, preheat the grill. Cook the poppadums under a hot grill, one at a time until they puff up and turn brown. They can burn in seconds so you must pay attention! Stack them up on top of one another to crisp and cool.
4. Mix the yogurt with the mint or coriander and ground cumin. Season to taste. Spoon the yogurt over the vegetables and serve from the wok. The poppadums can be crumbled on top of the dish.

Points per serving: 3½
Total Points per recipe: 14

Melon and Prawn Salad

Serves: 4

Preparation and cooking time:
10 minutes + 30 minutes marinating
Calories per serving: with Galia 85; with honeydew 90

Freezing: not recommended

Make sure the melon is just ripe and not too juicy or too sweet. Mango or pawpaw (papaya) could be used instead of melon. This salad is ideal for entertaining since it can be made an hour or two ahead.

1 small melon, e.g. Galia or honeydew, de-seeded and quartered
200 g (7 oz) shelled prawns, thawed if frozen
2 salad onions, sliced thinly
1 fresh red chilli, de-seeded and sliced thinly
2 tablespoons Thai fish sauce or light soy sauce
½ teaspoon caster sugar
juice of 1 lime
freshly ground black pepper
To serve:
dark green lettuce leaves
a few sprigs of fresh coriander or sweet Thai basil, chopped roughly

1. Slice the skin off the melon and cut the flesh into half moon slices.
2. Pat the prawns dry with kitchen paper and season with pepper.
3. Mix the onions, chilli, fish sauce or soy sauce, sugar and lime juice together by shaking them in a jar. Pour over the prawns and mix well. Leave to marinate in the fridge for about half an hour or so.
4. When ready to serve, toss in the melon slices and serve on small plates on which you have laid some dark green salad leaves. Scatter over the herb sprigs and eat quickly!

Points per serving: with Galia 1½; with honeydew 2½
Total Points per recipe: with Galia 6; with honeydew 10

Spicy Fish and Prawn Cakes

Serves: 4

Preparation and cooking time:
15 minutes
Calories per serving: 110

Freezing: recommended if fresh prawns are used

These fishcakes make a lovely starter served with salad or with sliced green beans tossed in a trickle of sesame oil and sprinkled with sesame seeds.

2 salad onions, chopped roughly
1 garlic clove, crushed
2 teaspoons ginger purée or grated fresh root ginger
1 fresh green chilli, de-seeded and chopped or 1 teaspoon chilli purée or grated fresh root ginger
250 g (9 oz) skinless, boneless cod or haddock fillets, cut into small chunks
125 g (4½ oz) peeled prawns, thawed if frozen
2 tablespoons Thai fish sauce or light soy sauce
1 teaspoon ground coriander
2 teaspoons sunflower oil
½ teaspoon salt (optional)
freshly ground black pepper, to taste
1 small lemon or lime, cut into wedges, to serve

1. Put the onions, garlic, ginger and chilli into a food processor and whizz for a few seconds until chopped finely.
2. Place the fish in the processor with the prawns, fish sauce or soy sauce, coriander and pepper.
3. Blend everything together until the mixture looks mashed and just begins to hold together. Do not over-process or you will end up with a purée.
4. Heat the oil in a large non-stick frying-pan and brush it all over the pan. Take a small spoonful of the mixture and fry it for a minute or so on each side, then cool and taste it. If you think it needs it, mix in ½ teaspoon of salt.
5. Using hands dipped into cold water, shape the mixture into eight patties. Reheat the pan. When the pan is hot cook the patties for 3 minutes on each side until they feel firm and are golden brown. Drain the patties on kitchen paper and serve garnished with the lemon or lime wedges.

Points per serving: 2
Total Points per recipe: 8

Chilli Prawn, Mange-tout Peas and Mango Salad

Serves: 2

Preparation and cooking time:
15 minutes
Calories per serving: 175

Freezing: not recommended

Fruit with seafood is a popular combination in Thai salads. Instead of a rich oil dressing which is full of Points and Calories, this salad has a light and scrumptious chilli and lime sauce.

1 mango, ripe but not soft
125 g (4½ oz) mange-tout peas, halved
8 tiger prawns or 125 g (4½ oz) large peeled prawns
For the dressing:
2 teaspoons soft brown sugar
2 tablespoons boiling hot water
1 large fresh red chilli, de-seeded and chopped
1 garlic clove, crushed
3 tablespoons Thai fish sauce or light soy sauce
juice of 1 lime
1 small stem of fresh lemon grass, chopped finely
2 tablespoons chopped fresh coriander
To serve:
a small handful of rocket or watercress leaves
2 salad onions, cut into thin strips

1. Take the mango and cut down each side of the flat central stone. Peel off the skin and slice the flesh thinly. Set aside.
2. Blanch the mange-tout peas in a little boiling salted water and then drain and rinse in cold running water. Pick over the prawns and check that they are peeled evenly.
3. Dissolve the sugar in the boiling hot water. Put this syrup in a jar with the rest of the dressing ingredients and shake them together.
4. Gently mix the mango, mange-tout peas and prawns with the dressing. Divide the salad leaves between two plates and pile the salad in the centre. Top with the shreds of salad onions.

Points per serving: 2½
Total Points per recipe: 5

Indian Crudités with Mango Curry Dip

Serves: 4

Preparation and cooking time: 15 minutes
Calories per serving: 140

Freezing: not recommended

Ⓥ

For dieters, the problem with many dips is that they tend to be creamy and high in fat. But a purée of onion combined with tangy mango chutney and very low-fat plain fromage frais gives you the same taste sensation without the extra Points and Calories.

2 carrots, cut into thin strips
1/3 cucumber, de-seeded, quartered lengthways and cut into strips
1 head of chicory, leaves separated
a handful of radishes, trimmed but some smaller leaves left on
a few sprigs of flat parsley, coriander or mint
For the dip:
1 onion, chopped
1 garlic clove, crushed
2 teaspoons sunflower oil
1 teaspoon mild or medium curry powder
2 teaspoons mango chutney
150 ml (1/4 pint) very low-fat plain fromage frais
1/2 teaspoon salt
freshly ground black pepper
To serve:
2 poppadums
1 low-fat flatbread (pitta size)

1. Chill the prepared vegetables until ready to serve.
2. For the dip, mix the onion, garlic and oil together in a small saucepan and gently cook for about 5 minutes until softened, stirring once or twice. Add the curry powder and dribbles of water if it starts sticking to the pan. Cook for a further minute.
3. Scoop the mixture into a food processor together with the chutney and fromage frais. Add the seasoning and whizz until smooth, scraping down at least once. Spoon into a suitable serving bowl.
4. Arrange the vegetables on a flat platter or small tray and scatter over the sprigs of herbs.
5. Grill the poppadums one at a time under a hot grill. Watch them like a hawk or they will surely burn. Break them into bite-sized pieces. Cut the flatbread into fingers. Arrange the poppadums and the flatbread fingers on a platter and stand the bowl of dip in the centre.

Points per serving: 2
Total Points per recipe: 8

Clear Japanese Vegetable Soup

Serves: 1

Preparation and cooking time: 5 minutes
Calories per serving: 20

Freezing: not recommended

Ⓥ

4 button mushrooms, sliced thinly
1 salad onion, chopped
1 small carrot, grated coarsely
a handful of watercress or lettuce shreds
8 g sachet of miso soup mix

Miso is a soya bean product so it is high in vegetable protein. You will find sachets of miso in health food stores and in many supermarkets.

1. Prepare all the vegetables. Remove any thick stalks of watercress or lettuce. Place the vegetables in a mug.
2. Tip in the contents of the miso sachet and top with boiling water. Stir well and drink!

Points per serving: 0
Total Points per recipe: 0

Seafood

In places like India, South-East Asia, China and Japan where there is plenty of coastline, it is hardly surprising that fish play such an important role in the native cuisine. And now fresh fish from the Orient are increasingly easy to find here in fishmongers although they are still rather expensive. Luckily however, many of the fish we know well are actually part of the same species as the Asian fish and can be used to achieve a taste which is very close to the real thing.

Sweet and Sour Tiger Prawns

Serves: 2

Preparation and cooking time:
15 minutes
Calories per serving: 155

Freezing: not recommended

Large, succulent prawns from South-East Asia are increasingly easy to find in fishmongers and supermarkets. Uncooked tiger prawns are ideal for this recipe; they will look translucent and pale grey at first but when you cook them, they will turn a beautiful pink colour in just minutes.

10 large tiger prawns, peeled
2 tablespoons light soy sauce
½ teaspoon Chinese five-spice powder
1 garlic clove, crushed
a small knob of fresh root ginger, chopped or 1 teaspoon ginger purée
2 teaspoons sunflower oil
5 cm (2-inch) piece of cucumber, cut in half lengthways and sliced thinly into half moons
½ small yellow pepper, de-seeded and sliced thinly
3 salad onions, chopped
sea salt and freshly ground black pepper
For the sauce:
2 tablespoons pineapple juice
1 tablespoon dry sherry
1 tablespoon rice wine or white wine vinegar
1 teaspoon caster sugar
4 tablespoons water
1 heaped teaspoon cornflour

1. Pick over the prawns. You may leave the tails on for effect, if you like. Mix them with one tablespoon of soy sauce, the five-spice powder, garlic and ginger. Leave them to marinate for 5 minutes or so while you prepare the vegetables. Mix all the sauce ingredients together and add the remaining tablespoon of soy sauce.
2. Heat the oil in a large wok or a non-stick frying-pan. Stir-fry the cucumber and pepper with the onions for a minute or two.
3. Add the prawns to the wok and stir-fry for about 2 minutes until they have all turned pink and feel firm when pressed.
4. Stir in the sauce and cook for a few seconds until it turns glossy and thickens. Check the seasoning and serve immediately.

Points per serving: 2½
Total Points per recipe: 5

Crab Foo Yung Omelette

Serves: 2

Preparation and cooking time:
15 minutes
Calories per serving: 195

Freezing: not recommended

Instead of crab, you could also
use peeled prawns or some
cooked, flaked white fish such
as cod or haddock.

125 g (4½ oz) white crab meat,
   thawed if frozen, drained if
   canned
2 tablespoons light soy sauce
1 teaspoon sweet chilli sauce
1 teaspoon sunflower oil
½ teaspoon sesame oil
2 salad onions, chopped
1 garlic clove, crushed or 1
   small teaspoon garlic purée
1 teaspoon ginger purée or
   grated fresh root ginger
2 eggs, beaten and seasoned
2 teaspoons chopped fresh
   coriander or parsley

1. Flake the crab and check for any pieces of shell. Mix with the soy
and chilli sauces.
2. In a small omelette pan, heat the two oils and when hot, stir-fry
the onions, garlic and ginger for a minute or two until softened.
3. Pour in the eggs and let the mixture set a little on the bottom,
then gently stir the pan contents and let the mixture set again.
4. Continue like this until most of the egg has set but is still a little
soft. Do not overstir. Add the crab and herbs and then tip the
omelette out of the pan, folding it in half.

Points per serving: 3½
Total Points per recipe: 7

Goan Spicy Fish in Coconut Sauce

Serves: 4

Preparation and cooking time:
20 minutes + 20 minutes
steeping
Calories per serving: 140

Freezing: recommended if
fresh fish is used

Coconut, chillies and fish are
very traditional ingredients in
Goan cuisine. Serve this dish
with basmati rice.

40 g (1½ oz) desiccated coconut
200 ml (7 fl oz) boiling water
2 large green or red chillies, de-
   seeded and chopped finely
2 garlic cloves, crushed
2 cm (¾-inch) piece of fresh
   root ginger, grated or 1
   tablespoon ginger purée
1 teaspoon ground turmeric
1 tablespoon ground coriander
1 teaspoon ground cumin
1 teaspoon freshly ground black
   pepper
1 teaspoon sea salt
1 tablespoon fresh lime juice
1 tablespoon sunflower oil
400 g (14 oz) firm white fish
   fillets, e.g. cod, haddock or
   monkfish, skinned and cut
   into bite-sized chunks
some chopped fresh parsley or
   coriander, to garnish

1. Steep the coconut in the boiling water and leave to cool until it
reaches room temperature (about 20 minutes). Strain the mixture,
pressing the coconut down with the back of a ladle. Discard the
coconut.
2. Mix the chillies with the garlic, ginger, ground spices, pepper,
salt and lime juice to form a paste.
3. Heat the oil in a large non-stick frying-pan and fry the spice paste
gently for a minute or two until softened. Pour in the coconut liquor
and bring to the boil. Bubble for 2 or 3 minutes until reduced a little.
4. Now add the fish chunks and gently stir once or twice during
cooking so they cook evenly. Simmer gently for up to 5 minutes but
do not overcook. Serve immediately sprinkled with some chopped
parsley or coriander.

Points per serving: 4
Total Points per recipe: 16

Pineapple and Prawn Thai Rice

Serves: 4

Preparation and cooking time: 20 minutes

Calories per serving: 265

Freezing: not recommended

This is a popular Thai rice dish which is sometimes served in a hollowed pineapple shell. Be sure to use lightly sticky Thai jasmine rice which has a natural fragrant aroma.

200 g (7 oz) Thai jasmine rice
2 teaspoons sunflower oil
2 garlic cloves, crushed
1 small onion, chopped
1 large fresh red chilli, de-seeded and sliced thinly
200 g (7 oz) fresh pineapple, chopped or canned pineapple in natural juice, drained
1 tablespoon Thai fish sauce
1 tablespoon light soy sauce
1 teaspoon sugar
75 g (2³/4 oz) peeled prawns, thawed if frozen
sea salt and freshly ground black pepper
2 tablespoons chopped fresh coriander or parsley, to serve

1. Boil the rice according to the pack instructions and then leave it to stand. Thai rice is slightly sticky – it will separate when stirred with the rest of the dish.
2. Heat the oil in a wok or large frying-pan and lightly fry the garlic, onion and chilli for 2 minutes, stirring occasionally. Add the pineapple and cook until reheated.
3. Mix in the fish sauce, soy sauce, sugar and prawns. Cook for a minute and then stir in the cooked rice. Reheat until piping hot and check the seasoning. Fork through the chopped herbs and serve.

Points per serving: 3¹/2
Total Points per recipe: 14

Chinese Red-cooked Salmon

Serves: 4

Preparation time: 10 minutes
+15 minutes marinating
+15 minutes cooking

Calories per serving: 195

Freezing: recommended if fresh salmon is used

'Red cooking' comes from the north of China where they like their food very spicy and hot. It appears red because of the spices used. Try to find the aromatic Sichuan red peppercorns in an Oriental food store since they lend such a nice authentic flavour.

4 × 100 g (3¹/2 oz) salmon fillets
For the marinade:
¹/2 teaspoon salt
1 teaspoon coarsely ground Sichuan peppercorns or ground mixed peppercorns
2 teaspoons ginger purée or grated fresh root ginger
1 garlic clove, crushed
¹/2 teaspoon mild chilli powder
¹/2 teaspoon Chinese five-spice powder
a pinch of ground cinnamon
2 tablespoons soy sauce
1 tablespoon dry sherry
1 teaspoon soft brown sugar
To serve:
2 salad onions, cut into thin shreds
¹/4 cucumber, halved lengthways, de-seeded and sliced thinly

1. Preheat the oven to Gas Mark 5/190°C/375°F. Pop the salmon fillets into a large food bag. Mix all the marinade ingredients together in a jug and then pour into the bag and rub into the fish. Leave to marinate for 15 minutes.
2. Remove the fish from the marinade and lay on a shallow ovenproof baking dish. Bake for 12–15 minutes until the flesh feels firm when pressed with the back of a fork. Serve garnished with the salad onions and cucumber.

Points per serving: 3¹/2
Total Points per recipe: 14

Tikka-style Monkfish

Serves: 3

Preparation and cooking time:
20 minutes + 30 minutes
marinating
Calories per serving: 90

Freezing: not recommended

Tikkas are chunky pieces of
food, normally chicken or
paneer (an Indian cheese)
marinated in a mild, spicy
marinade and then cooked
kebab-style. The flavours in
a tikka are aromatic but not
too hot and are perfect for
monkfish. Serve with pitta
bread or plain boiled rice and
remember to count the
Points.

300 g (10½ oz) filleted monkfish,
   cut into large bite-sized
   chunks
For the marinade:
3 tablespoons low-fat plain
   yogurt
2 garlic cloves, crushed
2 cm (¾-inch) piece of fresh
   root ginger, grated or 1
   tablespoon ginger purée
1 large fresh green chilli, de-
   seeded and chopped finely
¼ teaspoon ground black
   pepper
¼ teaspoon mild chilli powder
1 teaspoon ground turmeric
1 teaspoon ground cumin
½ teaspoon salt
a good pinch of ground nutmeg
a good pinch of dried mint
To serve:
fresh lemon or lime quarters
some chopped fresh mint
   leaves

1. Make sure that you trim any grey membrane from the monkfish
since it will cause the fish to curl when cooked. Put the monkfish
into a food bag.
2. Mix all the marinade ingredients together in a bowl and then
spoon into the monkfish bag and rub together well. Set aside to
marinate for about half an hour.
3. Preheat the grill to high. Thread the monkfish chunks on to 3
skewers and place under the grill. Turn the heat down to medium
and cook the fish for about 3–4 minutes on each side or until the
flesh feels firm when pressed with the back of a fork.
4. Serve hot, garnished with lemon or lime quarters and fresh mint.

Points per serving: 3
Total Points per recipe: 9

Steamed Fish with Soy Ginger Vegetables

Serves: 2

Preparation and cooking time:
20 minutes
Calories per serving: 150

Freezing: not recommended

The Chinese are very fond of
steaming their food. Here
fillets of plaice are steamed in
ramekins with finely sliced
vegetables and delicious
flavourings. Accompany with
plain, boiled rice.

1 small leek, sliced thinly
1 carrot, sliced very thinly
50 g (1¾ oz) mange-tout peas,
   sliced diagonally
2 × 100 g (3½ oz) skinned
   plaice fillets
1 tablespoon grated fresh root
   ginger
For the sauce:
1 teaspoon sesame oil
1 teaspoon garlic purée
1 salad onion, chopped finely
1 tablespoon light soy sauce
a pinch of caster sugar
salt and freshly ground black
   pepper

1. Blanch the leek, carrot and mange-tout peas in boiling water for
2 minutes, then drain and rinse in cold, running water. Divide the
vegetables between two large ramekins or small heatproof bowls.
2. Season the fish, fold each fillet in half and place on top of the
vegetables. Scatter the ginger on top.
3. Put a steamer on to boil. You can use a traditional Chinese
bamboo steamer fitted in a wok or a metal steamer.
4. Heat the sauce ingredients together in a small pan on the stove
or in a jug in the microwave and then pour it over the fish. Place
the ramekins in the steamer basket, cover with a lid and steam for
5–8 minutes or until the fish feels firm when pressed with the
back of a fork. Serve the fish in the ramekins or heatproof bowls.

Points per serving: 2
Total Points per recipe: 4

Spicy Indian Baked Mackerel

Serves: 4

Preparation and cooking time:
20 minutes + 30 minutes
standing
Calories per serving: 205

Freezing: not recommended

Serve with sliced tomatoes or
hot, crisp beans and rice or
warm pitta bread. Add the
extra Points for the rice and
bread.

2 × 300 g (10½ oz) mackerel,
  gutted and heads removed
juice of 1 small lemon
sea salt and freshly ground
  black pepper
For the spice paste:
2 fresh green chillies or 1
  teaspoon chilli paste
1 cm (½-inch) piece of fresh
  root ginger, grated
2 garlic cloves, crushed
½ small onion, chopped
25 g (1 oz) creamed coconut,
  softened or 1 small sachet of
  coconut powder
1 teaspoon mild or hot curry
  powder

1. Wash the insides of the fish well. Pat dry and then slash the flesh
twice on each side. Season lightly.
2. For the spice paste, put all the ingredients into a spice grinder or
food processor and whizz until smooth and creamy, scraping the
sides once or twice.
3. Spread this paste over the fish, including the insides. Cover and
leave for half an hour.
4. Preheat the oven to Gas Mark 5/190°C/375°F. Place the fish in a
shallow ovenproof dish and then bake for about 15–20 minutes
until the flesh feels firm when pressed with the back of a fork.
Remove from the oven and leave to stand for 5 minutes.
5. Season and sprinkle with the lemon juice. Serve hot.

Variation:
Whole trout is also good in this recipe. The Calories per serving
will be 175.

Points per serving: 5½
Total Points per recipe: 22

Bangkok Fish Curry

Serves: 4

**Preparation time: 15 minutes
+20 minutes steeping
+15 minutes cooking
Calories per serving: 130**

**Freezing: recommended if
fresh fish is used**

**Because Thailand has so many
inland waterways, not to
mention good coastlines, fish
is naturally a big feature in
Thai cooking.**

50 g (1¾ oz) desiccated
  coconut
300 ml (½ pint) boiling water
500 g (1 lb 2 oz) haddock or
  cod fillets, skinned and cut
  into large chunks
sea salt and freshly ground
  black pepper
For the paste:
1 small onion, chopped roughly
2 cm (¾-inch) piece of fresh
  root ginger, grated
2 dried kaffir lime leaves
  (optional)
1 fresh green chilli, de-seeded
  and chopped
a small handful of fresh
  coriander leaves
½ teaspoon ground cumin
½ teaspoon ground turmeric
½ teaspoon salt
To garnish:
1 fresh red chilli, de-seeded and
  sliced thinly (optional)
a few leaves of fresh basil

1. Steep the coconut in the boiling water and leave to cool until the
water reaches room temperature (about 20 minutes). Strain, pressing
down the coconut with the back of a spoon. Discard the coconut
and reserve the liquid.
2. To make the paste, put all the ingredients into a food processor
and whizz together until smooth. Slowly add a little of the coconut
water until you have a thick but runny purée. Reserve the rest of
the coconut water for the next step.
3. Spoon this mixture into a medium-size saucepan and bring to
the boil, stirring once or twice. Simmer for a minute and then stir
in the rest of the coconut water. Return to a simmer.
4. Drop the fish pieces in one by one and cook gently for just
5 minutes. Check the seasoning and serve garnished with a few
slices of red chilli (if using) and the basil leaves.

Points per serving: 4½
Total Points per recipe: 18

Meat and Poultry

Indian, Chinese and Thai cuisines have become so popular that you can now buy a whole range of ready-made sauces in supermarkets. If you are trying to lose weight you should avoid those that are high in Points and Calories. In any case you don't need to rely on them to prepare a quick meal; although the lists of ingredients may seem rather long and daunting in Asian recipes, many ingredients are dried or bottled spices which are already in your storecupboard. Once you've measured them out, the cooking is easy!

Punjabi Lamb Chops

Serves: 4

Preparation time: 10 minutes
+45 minutes cooking
Calories per serving: 310

Freezing: recommended

This is a rich, warming and delicious lamb dish from the Punjab (the land of five rivers). Serve with spinach and rice or mashed potatoes.

4 lean lamb chump chops, trimmed
1 onion, sliced
2 teaspoons sunflower oil
1 teaspoon cumin seeds or ground cumin
½ teaspoon ground cinnamon
½ teaspoon ground turmeric
½ teaspoon ground chilli (optional)
2 cm (³/₄-inch) piece of fresh root ginger, grated
3 tomatoes, skinned and chopped
1 large fresh green chilli or 1 teaspoon chilli purée
300 ml (½ pint) stock or water
sea salt and freshly ground black pepper

1. Preheat the oven to Gas Mark 4/180°C/350°F. Heat a non-stick pan until very hot and then quickly seal the chops on each side until browned. Put them in a casserole dish.
2. Add the onion and oil to the pan and sauté gently for up to 5 minutes until softened. Add the cumin, cinnamon, turmeric and chilli (if using) and fry for a minute to release the aroma. Then stir in the ginger, tomatoes and fresh chilli and cook for about 3 minutes. Add the stock and boil for 2 minutes, season and then pour the sauce over the chops.
3. Cover and bake for up to 45 minutes until the meat feels tender when prodded with a fork.

Points per serving: 4
Total Points per recipe: 16

Keema (Indian Mince with Peas)

Serves: 4

Preparation time: 10 minutes
+20 minutes cooking
Calories per serving: 295

Freezing: recommended

This is India's answer to Bolognese sauce! Top with some low-fat plain yogurt and serve with plain boiled potatoes or rice, adding the extra Points.

2 teaspoons sunflower oil
500 g (1 lb 2 oz) extra-lean beef mince
2 garlic cloves or 2 teaspoons garlic purée
2 cm (³/₄-inch) piece of fresh root ginger, grated or 1 teaspoon ginger purée
1 onion, chopped finely
1–2 tablespoons curry powder, to taste
2 whole cloves
½ teaspoon ground cinnamon
300 ml (½ pint) stock or water
1 tablespoon mango chutney, chopped if chunky
125 g (4½ oz) frozen peas, thawed
sea salt and freshly ground black pepper

1. Heat the oil in a large non-stick frying-pan and brown the mince, stirring well until it is crumbly.
2. Add the garlic, ginger and onion and continue frying gently for 5 minutes until softened. Stir in the curry powder and cook for a further minute, then mix in the cloves and cinnamon.
3. Add the stock or water, chutney and some seasoning. Bring to the boil, then cover and simmer for 10 minutes. Uncover and stir in the peas. Cook for 2–3 minutes.

Points per serving: 4½
Total Points per recipe: 18

Lamb Jalfrezi

Serves: 4

Preparation time: 10 minutes
+1 hour cooking
Calories per serving: 210

Freezing: recommended

A Jalfrezi is hot and spicy and
full of colourful sliced peppers
and onions. For the best
flavour, make this one day in
advance and then scrape off
any fat that solidifies on top.

400 g (14 oz) lean stewing lamb
  (leg shank or neck fillet), well
  trimmed and diced
1 teaspoon cumin seeds
2 teaspoons sunflower oil
1 onion, sliced thinly
2 garlic cloves, chopped finely
2 cm (³/4-inch) piece of fresh
  root ginger or 1 teaspoon
  ginger purée
1 large green chilli, de-seeded
  and chopped
1 teaspoon ground paprika
¹/2 teaspoon hot chilli powder
  or more, to taste
¹/2 teaspoon ground turmeric
1 red pepper, de-seeded and
  sliced thinly
1 small yellow or green pepper,
  de-seeded and sliced thinly
4 tomatoes, skinned and
  chopped
150 ml (¹/4 pint) stock or water
2 tablespoons chopped fresh
  coriander (optional)
sea salt and freshly ground
  black pepper

1. Preheat the oven to Gas Mark 4/180°C/350°F. Heat a large non-stick frying-pan and when hot, brown the diced lamb on all sides for about 5 minutes. Remove to a casserole dish.
2. Sprinkle the cumin seeds into the pan and cook for a few seconds to release their aroma. Then add the oil, onion, garlic, ginger and chilli. Stir and cook gently for 3 minutes, then mix in the paprika, hot chilli powder and turmeric. Cook for another minute.
3. Add the sliced peppers and chopped tomatoes and continue cooking for 5 minutes until softened, adding the stock or water towards the end of the 5 minutes. Season well and pour the sauce over the lamb.
4. Cover and bake for about 50 minutes or until the lamb is tender. Stir in the chopped coriander (if using).

Variation:
Skinned, boneless chicken thighs can be used instead to make a Chicken Jalfrezi. This will reduce the Points per serving to 2¹/2. Calories per serving will be 170.

Points per serving: 6
Total Points per recipe: 24

Paper-steamed Aromatic Chicken

Serves: 1

Preparation time: 15 minutes
+ marinating +15 minutes
cooking
Calories per serving: 165

Freezing: not recommended

As this recipe demonstrates,
steaming is a wonderful way
to keep a chicken breast moist
and retain as much of the
natural flavour as possible.
This is delicious with Thai
jasmine rice or basmati.

100 g (3¹/2 oz) skinless, boneless
  chicken breast
1 small leek, shredded or 2
  salad onions, sliced finely
¹/2 teaspoon sesame oil
1 star anise or a good pinch of
  Chinese five-spice powder
¹/2 teaspoon ground coriander
1 tablespoon dry sherry
1 tablespoon light soy sauce
sea salt and freshly ground
  black pepper

1. Slash the chicken breast 2 or 3 times and season. Place in the middle of a sheet of greaseproof paper, large enough to wrap the chicken in.
2. Blanch the leek or salad onions for 2 minutes in a little water or microwave until limp. Drain and toss with the sesame oil.
3. Put some water in a steaming pan or wok (if you have one with a trivet, cover and basket) and put it on to boil.
4. Place the star anise on top of the chicken or sprinkle it with the five-spice powder. Add the coriander, sherry and soy sauce. Season lightly again.
5. Wrap the paper around the chicken like a parcel, double-folding the top and tucking the ends underneath. Place on the steaming basket. Cover and steam for 12–15 minutes depending on the thickness of the breast. The breast is cooked if it feels firm when pressed with the back of a fork.
6. Remove from the steamer and leave to rest for 5 minutes. Then unwrap carefully and tip the chicken, leek and juices on to a plate.

Points per serving: 3

Turkey Korma

Serves: 2

Preparation time: 10 minutes
+ 15 minutes cooking
Calories per serving: 230

Freezing: recommended if
fresh turkey is used

According to legend, a Korma
should be made with white
foods only and then eaten by
moonlight in white clothes.
In favour of reducing the
Calories, we break with
tradition here and use
alternatives to the usual
cream and butter!

1 garlic clove, chopped roughly
1 small onion, chopped
2 tablespoons skimmed milk
2 teaspoons sunflower
  margarine
200 g (7 oz) boneless turkey cut
  into stir-fry strips
1–2 teaspoons korma spice
  powder or mild curry powder
1 tablespoon ground almonds
50 g (1³/₄ oz) half-fat crème
  fraîche
sea salt and freshly ground
  black pepper
a small handful of fresh
  coriander sprigs, to garnish

1. Put the garlic, onion and milk in a food processor or liquidiser
and process to make a paste. This is not essential but it does give
the traditional texture of a korma. If you prefer, you can just chop
the garlic and onion very finely.
2. Melt the margarine in a non-stick pan and gently sauté the
turkey until just firm. Remove and set aside. Add the onion paste
to the pan and cook gently for 2 minutes until softened.
3. Return the turkey to the pan and sprinkle in the korma spice
powder or mild curry powder and almonds. Season and cook for
another 3 minutes. Stir in the crème fraîche and return to a simmer.
Check the seasoning and serve, sprinkled with coriander sprigs.

Points per serving: 4¹/₂
Total Points per recipe: 9

Tandoori-roasted Chicken with Minty Yogurt Dip

Serves: 3

Preparation time: 10 minutes
+ marinating + 45 minutes
cooking
Calories per serving: 610

Freezing: recommended if
fresh chicken is used

The tandoor is a traditional
clay oven from northern India.
Tender meats are marinated
first in yogurt and spices and
then cooked quickly at very
high temperatures to give a
char-grilled taste and succulent
texture. Tandoori food is
usually served with naan
bread which can be high in
fat, but pitta bread makes a
good substitute.

1.25 kg (2 lb 12 oz) roasting
  chicken
2 teaspoons tandoori spice mix
a good pinch of garlic powder or
  1 small garlic clove, crushed
300 ml (¹/₂ pint) low-fat plain
  yogurt
¹/₄ cucumber, grated coarsely
2 tablespoons chopped fresh
  mint
a good pinch of dried dill
1 lemon, quartered
sea salt and freshly ground
  black pepper

1. Prepare the chicken, untrussing it if necessary. Pull out any pads
of fat from the body cavity. Trim the legs and make a few cuts in the
breast and legs. Season the flesh. Put the chicken into a roasting bag.
2. Mix the spice mix with the garlic and half the yogurt. Spoon this
mixture into the bag with the chicken and rub together well. Seal
loosely and leave to marinate for at least one hour.
3. Preheat the oven to Gas Mark 7/220°C/425°F. Give the chicken
in the bag one more rub and, still in its bag, place in a shallow
roasting-pan. Pierce the bag once at the top.
4. Roast for about 45 minutes. Check if it is cooked by untying and
piercing the section between the thigh and the body. If any pink
juices run out and the flesh looks pink, then return to cook for a
few more minutes.
5. Meanwhile, make the dip. Mix the remaining yogurt with the
cucumber, mint, dill and seasoning. Spoon into a bowl. Chill.
6. Let the chicken rest in its bag for 10 minutes. Then pour off any
juices into a gravy jug, allowing any fat to settle on top and then
spoon off carefully. Cut the bird into portions with kitchen scissors
and spoon over the pan juices. Serve with the dip and lemon
quarters.

Points per serving: 4¹/₂
Total Points per recipe: 13¹/₂

Beef Teriyaki

Serves: 2

Preparation and cooking time:
25 minutes + 30 minutes
marinating
Calories per serving: 190

Freezing: not recommended

Japanese food is finally
becoming popular in the West.
This is good news for dieters
since it is a very lean and
healthy cuisine which is full
of flavour.

200 g (7 oz) lean beef steak, e.g.
   fillet or rump, trimmed of
   any fat
1 tablespoon sake or very dry
   sherry
3 tablespoons dark Japanese
   soy sauce + extra for serving
2 tablespoons mirin or 1
   tablespoon medium sherry
   or vermouth
1/4 cucumber, quartered
   lengthways, de-seeded and
   sliced thinly
1/4 small white cabbage,
   shredded finely
2 carrots, grated coarsely or
   shredded finely
a little hot mustard and cress,
   to garnish

1. Place the beef in a food bag. Mix the sake, soy sauce and mirin
in a cup and then tip into the food bag and rub into the meat. Seal
and leave to marinate for 30 minutes.
2. Heat a heavy-based, non-stick frying-pan, preferably ridged, and
when very hot, remove the beef from the food bag and cook for
about 3–5 minutes on each side. It should be just done but the
timing will depend on the thickness of the meat and how well you
like your meat cooked.
3. Meanwhile, arrange the cucumber, cabbage and carrots in neat
piles on two plates. Garnish with a little cress. Pour extra soy sauce
into two dainty bowls and place these on the plate too.
4. Remove the beef from the pan and leave to stand for 4–5 minutes,
then slice thinly. Divide the slices between the plates and serve
immediately.

Points per serving: 3 1/2
Total Points per recipe: 7

Balti Meatballs

Serves: 4

Preparation and cooking time:
15 minutes
Calories per serving: with beef
270; with turkey 185

Freezing: recommended

**Balti cooking is now very
fashionable. This is a great
family meal. Serve with pitta
bread and remember to count
the Points.**

1 teaspoon sea salt
2 teaspoons garam masala or
   mild curry powder
1/2 teaspoon garlic powder
500 g (1 lb 2 oz) extra-lean
   minced beef or turkey
2 teaspoons sunflower oil
For the sauce:
1 onion, chopped roughly
2 garlic cloves
1 fresh green chilli, de-seeded
   and chopped roughly
1/2 teaspoon cumin seeds
4 tomatoes, skinned and
   chopped
2–3 tablespoons low-fat plain
   yogurt, stirred
1 tablespoon chopped fresh
   mint
sea salt and freshly ground
   black pepper

1. Make sure your hands are clean. Mix together the salt, garam
masala spice, garlic powder and some black pepper and stir well into
the mince. Divide and shape the mixture into 8 balls, periodically
rinsing your hands in cold water so the meat doesn't stick.
2. Heat the oil in a non-stick frying-pan and fry the meatballs,
shaking the pan occasionally so the meatballs take on a neat round
shape. Cook for about 5 minutes and then remove and drain on
kitchen paper.
3. Meanwhile, process the onion, fresh garlic and chilli in a food
processor to make a purée. Add this to the pan and cook gently
for about 3 minutes. Then stir in the cumin seeds and cook for
another minute.
4. Mix in the tomatoes and 150 ml (1/4 pint) water plus seasoning
to taste. Bring to the boil and cook for 2 minutes, squashing the
tomatoes slightly. Then return the meatballs to the pan, cover, and
cook for 10 minutes. Serve in a shallow dish with the stirred yogurt
trickled over. Sprinkle with the chopped mint.

Points per serving: with beef 5; with turkey 4 1/2
Total Points per recipe: with beef 20; with turkey 18

Marinated Duck Breasts

Serves: 2

Preparation and cooking time:
20 minutes + 30 minutes
marinating
Calories per serving: 270

Freezing: not recommended

Although duck breasts are
sold with the fatty skin still
on, it is quite simple to pull
or cut it off, leaving a dark
and delicious lean meat.
Duck is a traditional meat in
Thailand and Indonesia.

2 × 150 g (5½ oz) duck breasts,
   fat removed
2 tablespoons dark soy sauce
½ teaspoon freshly ground
   black pepper
grated zest and juice of 1 lime
1 teaspoon sunflower oil
2 garlic cloves, sliced thinly
75 g (2¾ oz) button
   mushrooms or 50 g (1¾ oz)
   shiitake mushrooms, sliced
1 tablespoon Thai fish sauce
sea salt and freshly ground
   black pepper
To serve:
1 salad onion, cut into thin
   shreds
a few sprigs of watercress

1. Slash the duck breasts in 2 or 3 places. Mix the soy sauce, pepper,
lime zest and juice and pour into a food bag. Pop in the duck breasts,
rub in the marinade and leave to marinate for 30 minutes or so.
Remove and shake dry.
2. Heat a heavy-based non-stick frying-pan until hot and cook the
duck breasts for about 5 minutes on each side until slightly springy
when pressed. If you like duck well done, then allow extra time.
Remove the duck and lower the heat.
3. Add the oil to the pan and fry the sliced garlic until lightly
browned. Then stir in the mushrooms, 3 tablespoons of water and
the fish sauce. Check the seasoning and cook for 2 minutes, stirring
constantly.
4. Slice the duck breasts on the diagonal and place on two plates.
Spoon over the garlic and mushrooms and garnish with the onion
shreds and watercress sprigs.

Points per serving: 3½
Total Points per recipe: 7

Chinese Marinated Ribs with Five Spices

Serves: 4

Preparation time: 5 minutes
+ marinating +1 hour cooking
Calories per serving: with pork
295; with lamb 385

Freezing: recommended

The Chinese have a saying –
the nearer the bone, the
sweeter the meat. But short-
cut 'spare ribs' which are
quite lean can also be quite
tough if cooked too quickly.
The secret is to cook them
slowly at a low temperature
and pour away any fat that
seeps out.

1 kg (2 lb 4 oz) pork or lamb
   spare ribs, chopped into
   13 cm (5-inch) lengths
½ teaspoon sea salt
½ teaspoon freshly ground
   Sichuan red or black
   peppercorns
3 tablespoons dark soy sauce
2 tablespoons dry sherry
1 tablespoon wine vinegar
2 tablespoons Chinese plum
   sauce or chutney
1 tablespoon honey
1 teaspoon garlic purée or
   ½ teaspoon garlic powder
1 teaspoon ginger purée
1 teaspoon Chinese five-spice
   powder
1 small onion, chopped finely
slices of lemon, to serve

1. As far as possible trim the spare ribs of any visible fat. Place in a
large food bag.
2. Mix all the other ingredients together in a jug and then pour
this marinade over the ribs. Make sure it is rubbed well on to the
ribs. Seal and leave in the fridge to marinate for at least ½ hour,
preferably overnight.
3. Preheat the oven to Gas Mark 3/170°C/325°F. Shake the ribs out
into a roasting pan. Cover loosely with foil and bake for 45 minutes,
stirring once or twice. Increase the temperature to Gas Mark
6/200°C/400°F and cook for at least another 15–20 minutes or
until the ribs turn syrupy and the meat can be pulled off the bone
easily. Hand napkins round the table and serve with small finger
bowls of warm water and slices of lemon.

Points per serving: 5½
Total Points per recipe: 22

Spiced Chicken Patties

Serves: 4

Preparation and cooking time:
20 minutes
Calories per serving: 235

Freezing: recommended

Here is India's version of
burgers. They are simple to
make and cook in minutes so
they are perfect for after work.

1 small onion, grated
500 g (1 lb 2 oz) lean minced
    chicken or turkey
2 garlic cloves, crushed or
    2 teaspoons garlic purée
2 teaspoons ginger purée or
    grated fresh root ginger
1 tablespoon tikka spice mix
    or mild curry powder
1 teaspoon salt
low-fat cooking spray
juice of 1 small lemon or lime
To serve:
4 small pitta breads
1 Little Gem lettuce, shredded
4 tablespoons raita dip or low-
    fat plain yogurt
a few sprigs of fresh mint,
    chopped roughly
salt and freshly ground black
    pepper

1. Mix the grated onion, chicken or turkey, garlic, ginger, tikka
spice mix or curry powder and salt in a bowl and mix together
thoroughly. Shape into 8 patties or small burgers. If the meat sticks
to your fingers, simply dip your hands in cold water.
2. Spray a non-stick pan with low-fat cooking spray and, when hot,
cook the patties for about 3–5 minutes on each side until they feel
firm when pressed. Trickle over the lemon or lime juice while they
finish cooking.
3. Meanwhile, warm the pittas in the oven and then split and fill
them with the shredded lettuce. Pop two patties into each pitta,
spoon over some raita or yogurt. Season and scatter with mint.

Variation:
Instead of the raita dip or low-fat plain yogurt you could use the
minty dip from Tandoori-roasted Chicken (page 36). The Points
will remain the same.

Points per serving: 5 (for 2 patties)
Total Points per recipe: 20

Simple Sukiyaki

Serves: 2

Preparation and cooking time:
25 minutes
Calories per serving: 455

Freezing: not recommended

During the winter in Japan,
families gather around the
table to enjoy this dish of
thinly sliced beef and
prepared vegetables. Fun to
eat with chopsticks!

100 g (3½ oz) rice noodles
low-fat cooking spray
200 g (7 oz) sirloin steak,
    trimmed of fat and cut into
    thin slices
100 g (3½ oz) smoked or
    marinated tofu, cut into thin
    bite-sized pieces
1 leek, trimmed and cut
    diagonally into 1 cm (½-inch)
    slices
1 carrot, sliced thinly and
    diagonally
6 large button mushrooms or
    fresh shiitake mushrooms
3 large Chinese leaves, torn
    into pieces
For the sauce:
4 tablespoons light soy sauce
2 tablespoons mirin or
    medium-dry sherry
2 tablespoons sake (optional)
1 tablespoon caster sugar

1. Cook and drain the noodles according to the pack instructions.
Set aside.
2. Put the sauce ingredients in a small pot and heat until the sugar
has dissolved, stirring frequently. Pour into a jug.
3. Heat a large non-stick frying-pan and when hot, spray with low-
fat cooking spray.
4. Add the steak, tofu, leek, carrot, mushrooms and Chinese
leaves. Spoon the sauce over the vegetables.
5. Add the noodles to the pan. Continue to cook until the vegetables
are tender. Serve immediately.

Points per serving: 7½
Total Points per recipe: 15

Massaman Beef Curry

Serves: 4

Preparation time: 15 minutes
+20 minutes steeping
+1¼ hours braising
Calories per serving: 245

Freezing: recommended

The red curry paste used in Thai cooking creates lovely dark red and delicious stews. If you prefer a milder taste, use larger red chillies. This recipe is even tastier made the day before. Just scrape off any fat that settles and reheat.

For the curry paste:
1 small red onion, chopped
3 garlic cloves, chopped
3 fresh red chillies, de-seeded and chopped
2 cm (¾-inch) piece of fresh galangal, peeled and chopped or 1 teaspoon dried galangal
1 fresh lemon grass stem, chopped
2 teaspoons ground coriander
½ teaspoon cumin seeds
1 teaspoon salt
1 tablespoon Thai fish sauce
For the curry:
25 g (1 oz) desiccated coconut
400 ml (14 fl oz) boiling water
1 teaspoon sunflower oil
2 garlic cloves, chopped
500 g (1 lb 2 oz) lean braising beef, cubed
1 fresh red chilli, sliced diagonally (optional)
1 tablespoon chopped fresh basil
salt and freshly ground black pepper

1. Mix the coconut and boiling water together and leave to cool until it reaches room temperature (about 20 minutes). Then drain, squeezing the coconut with the back of a wooden spoon. Reserve the liquid and discard the coconut.
2. For the curry paste, blend all the ingredients to a chunky purée in a food processor. Do not overblend.
3. For the curry, heat the oil in a large saucepan and fry the garlic until browned. Stir in half the curry paste and cook for 2 minutes. Store the rest of the curry paste in a screw-top jar in the fridge for another time.
4. Stir in the beef and then add the coconut liquid, red chilli (if using) and seasoning. Bring to the boil, then cover and simmer very gently for 1 to 1¼ hours until tender. Stir in the basil leaves and serve hot.

Points per serving: 7
Total Points per recipe: 28

Thai Green Chicken Curry

Serves: 4

Preparation time: 10 minutes
+ 20 minutes steeping
+ 15 minutes cooking
Calories per serving: 145

Freezing: recommended

Thai curries are ideal for a weight-loss programme because the meat is stirred into a simmering stock with fresh spices and poached instead of fried. Serve with Thai jasmine rice.

For the paste:
3 large fresh green chillies, de-seeded and chopped
4 garlic cloves, chopped
1 large stem of lemon grass
3 kaffir lime leaves, or bay leaves, torn
1 teaspoon ground coriander
½ teaspoon cumin seeds
2 cm (¾-inch) cube of fresh galangal, peeled and chopped or 1 teaspoon dried
3 tablespoons fresh coriander leaves
1 teaspoon salt
2 tablespoons fresh lemon juice
For the curry:
25 g (1 oz) desiccated coconut
300 ml (½ pint) boiling water
1 teaspoon sunflower oil
1 large garlic clove, sliced thinly
75 g (2¾ oz) baby corn, halved diagonally
4 medium boneless, skinless chicken thighs, trimmed of fat and cubed
6 large leaves of fresh basil
salt and freshly ground black pepper

1. Steep the coconut in the boiling water and leave to cool until the water reaches room temperature (about 20 minutes). Drain, pressing down the pulp with the back of a spoon. Reserve the liquid and discard the coconut.
2. For the paste, grind all the ingredients together with a large pestle and mortar, or blend them to a chunky purée in a food processor. Do not overblend.
3. Heat the oil in a large saucepan. Fry the garlic in the oil until nicely browned and then stir in half the curry paste and cook for 2 minutes. Store the rest of the paste in a screw-top jar in the fridge for another time. It will keep for a week.
4. Add the coconut liquid, bring to the boil and drop in the baby corns and chicken cubes. Simmer, uncovered, for 15 minutes. Check the seasoning and add the basil leaves.

Cook's note:
You could also use a ready-made paste.

Points per serving: 2½
Total Points per recipe: 10

Pork Vindaloo

Serves: 4

Preparation time: 10 minutes
+ 30–40 minutes cooking
Calories per serving: 230

Freezing: recommended

Vindaloo curries are always hot and tangy. The best accompaniments for this dish are rice and raita (a refreshing mixture of yogurt with cucumber and mint).

1 onion, grated
2 garlic cloves, crushed
2 cm (¾-inch) piece of fresh root ginger, grated
1 tablespoon hot curry powder
1 teaspoon hot chilli powder
½ teaspoon freshly ground black pepper
2 teaspoons sunflower oil
400 g (14 oz) lean pork tenderloin, cubed
200 g (7 oz) potato, diced
2 tablespoons tomato paste
1 tablespoon wine vinegar
450 ml (16 fl oz) stock or water
2 tablespoons chopped fresh coriander
sea salt

1. First make a spice paste by mixing together the grated onion, garlic, ginger, curry and chilli powders and pepper. Heat a non-stick saucepan and add the oil.
2. Cook the pork cubes quickly in hot oil until browned and then stir in the paste and cook for a further minute. Add the potato.
3. Stir in the tomato paste, vinegar, stock or water and salt to taste. Bring to the boil, then cover and simmer gently for 30–40 minutes until the meat is tender and the potatoes are absorbed into the sauce. Stir in the coriander and serve.

Points per serving: 5½
Total Points per recipe: 22

Rice and Noodles

Rice and noodles are an essential part of the Asian food culture; in fact, Asians eat one or the other at almost every meal. Rice and noodles are ideal for those on a diet because they provide lots of energy and have very little fat. And of course there are so many interesting varieties to choose from now. Good basmati or Thai jasmine rice are excellent with Asian dishes because they have a wonderful natural aroma which adds a lovely flavour to a meal. And noodles are available in all shapes and sizes; be sure to try some rice or buckwheat noodles.

Rice Noodles with Broccoli and Prawns

Serves: 2

Preparation and cooking time: 20 minutes + 20 minutes soaking
Calories per serving: 340

Freezing: not recommended

125 g (4^1/$_2$ oz) rice noodles
1 garlic clove, crushed or 1 small teaspoon garlic purée
1 cm (^{1}/$_2$-inch) piece of fresh root ginger, grated or 1 tablespoon ginger purée
1 red chilli, de-seeded and sliced thinly
2 teaspoons sunflower oil

125 g (4^1/$_2$ oz) broccoli florets, sliced
4 tablespoons stock or water
100 g (3^1/$_2$ oz) peeled prawns, thawed and patted dry if frozen
1 salad onion, chopped
sea salt and freshly ground black pepper
For the sauce:
1 teaspoon sweet chilli sauce
2 tablespoons light soy sauce
a pinch of sugar
1 teaspoon rice wine vinegar or wine vinegar
^{1}/$_2$ teaspoon sesame oil

1. Soak the noodles in boiling water according to the pack instructions. Drain. Mix the sauce ingredients in a cup.
2. In a wok or large frying-pan fry the garlic, ginger and chilli in the oil for about 1 minute. Add the broccoli and stock or water. Bring to the boil, stirring as you would a stir-fry. Cover the pan and cook for a further 2 minutes, then mix in the prawns, salad onion and noodles. Season. Reheat until hot and bubbling and stir in the sauce.
3. Cook for another minute or two.

Points per serving: 5
Total Points per recipe: 10

Yellow Vegetable Pilaff

Serves: 4

Preparation time: 10 minutes + 20 minutes cooking
Calories per serving: 215

Freezing: recommended

Ⓥ

You can vary the vegetables in this recipe as long as they are all cut to the same size, but make sure you use easy-cook basmati rice so that the grains retain their texture.

1 small red onion, chopped
1 garlic clove, crushed
1 small red pepper, de-seeded and chopped
1 carrot, grated coarsely
2 teaspoons sunflower oil
175 g (6 oz) easy-cook basmati rice
1 teaspoon ground turmeric
^{1}/$_2$ teaspoon ground cumin
2 tablespoons light soy sauce
100 g (3^1/$_2$ oz) green beans, chopped
400 ml (14 fl oz) water
sea salt and freshly ground black pepper

1. Mix the onion, garlic, pepper and carrot with the oil. Put into a heavy-based saucepan with 3 tablespoons of water. Heat until the contents start to sizzle, then cover and turn the heat down. Cook for 5 minutes until softened.
2. Stir in the rice, cook for a minute and then mix in the turmeric and cumin. Cook for another minute. Add the soy sauce, green beans, water and seasoning. Bring to the boil, then cover and simmer gently for 15 minutes: do not lift the lid during cooking.
3. Leave the pan to stand for 5 minutes. Then uncover and separate the grains gently with a fork.

Points per serving: 3
Total Points per recipe: 12

Fragrant Rice on Chilli-dressed Lettuce

Serves: 4

Preparation and cooking time:
20 minutes
Calories per serving: 380

Freezing: not recommended

Ⓥ

Thais love salads like this in which hot food is tossed into chilled leaves.

175 g (6 oz) Thai fragrant or jasmine rice
300 ml (1/2 pint) water
1 lemon grass stem
1/4 iceberg lettuce, torn into bite-sized pieces
a small bag of rocket leaves
2 salad onions, sliced diagonally
sea salt and freshly ground black pepper
For the dressing:
2 teaspoons sunflower oil
1 tablespoon rice wine vinegar
1 tablespoon light soy sauce or fish sauce
1/2 teaspoon caster sugar
1 teaspoon sweet chilli sauce

1. Put the rice, water and lemon grass into a pan. Bring to the boil and then turn the heat right down. Cover and cook gently for 10 minutes without lifting the lid. Remove from the heat, still covered, and leave to stand for 5 minutes.
2. Toss together the pieces of iceberg lettuce, the rocket leaves and half the salad onions. Season to taste.
3. Shake the dressing ingredients together in a small jar and then toss into the salad. Tip this on to a platter. Spoon the rice on top, breaking it up lightly with a fork. It will be slightly sticky. Remove the lemon grass stem and scatter over the remaining onions. Serve immediately.

Points per serving: 3
Total Points per recipe: 12

Pork and Rice Stir-fry

Serves: 2

Preparation time: 10 minutes
+ marinating + 15 minutes
cooking
Calories per serving: 405

Freezing: recommended

For a change, you could substitute the rice with rice noodles.

200 g (7 oz) lean minced pork
1 tablespoon soy sauce
1 tablespoon dry sherry
1 teaspoon garlic purée
1 teaspoon ginger purée
1 teaspoon sweet chilli sauce
100 g (3 1/2 oz) long-grain rice
1 teaspoon sesame oil
2 teaspoons sunflower oil
2 salad onions, sliced diagonally
1 teaspoon cornflour blended with 5 tablespoons water
2 tablespoons chopped fresh coriander or parsley
sea salt and freshly ground black pepper

1. Mix the pork with the soy sauce, sherry, garlic and ginger purée and the chilli sauce. Set aside for 10 minutes.
2. Meanwhile, boil the rice according to the pack instructions. Drain and toss with the sesame oil.
3. Heat the sunflower oil in a non-stick wok or large-frying pan and then stir-fry the marinated mince for about 5 minutes until browned and crumbly.
4. Stir in the onions, cornflour mixture and seasoning. Bring to the boil and cook for 2 minutes. Mix in the rice and reheat. Sprinkle with chopped coriander or parsley and serve.

Variation:
Try minced turkey instead of pork. This will reduce the Points per serving to 7 1/2. Calories will be 390 per serving.

Points per serving: 8
Total Points per recipe: 16

Dan Dan Noodles

Serves: 4

Preparation and cooking time:
20 minutes
Calories per serving: 210

Freezing: not recommended

This popular Chinese noodle
dish comes from the northern
province of Sichuan.

200 g (7 oz) Chinese egg thread
    noodles
1 teaspoon sunflower oil
2 garlic cloves, crushed
2 cm (³/₄-inch) piece of fresh
    root ginger or 2 teaspoons
    ginger purée
1 dessertspoon dry sherry
1 dessertspoon chilli bean
    sauce
1 teaspoon peanut butter
1 tablespoon light soy sauce
1 teaspoon caster sugar
300 ml (¹/₂ pint) chicken stock
sea salt and freshly ground
    black pepper
a good pinch of sesame seeds,
    to serve

1. Prepare the Chinese egg noodles according to the pack instructions.
Drain and set aside.
2. In a small pan, mix together the oil, garlic and ginger. Heat for
2 minutes until softened and cooked, and then stir in the sherry,
chilli bean sauce, peanut butter, soy sauce and sugar. Cook for a
minute and then stir in the stock.
3. Bring to the boil and simmer for 2 minutes. Mix in the noodles
and check the seasoning. Serve immediately sprinkled lightly with
sesame seeds.

Points per serving: 3¹/₂
Total Points per recipe: 14

Thai Coconut and Lemon Grass Rice

Serves: 4

Preparation time: 10 minutes
+ 20 minutes steeping
Calories per serving: 350

Freezing: not recommended

(v)

Fragrant Thai rice cooked in
coconut-flavoured water is a
classic side dish for a Thai
meal. Serve unseasoned.

400 ml (14 fl oz) boiling water
25 g (1 oz) desiccated coconut
200 g (7 oz) Thai fragrant or
    jasmine rice
1 fresh lemon grass stem
1–2 dried Thai kaffir lime
    leaves (optional)

1. Pour the boiling water on to the coconut. Leave until water has
cooled to room temperature (about 20 minutes) and then strain,
pressing down the coconut with the back of a ladle. Discard the
coconut and reserve the liquid.
2. Mix together the coconut liquid, rice, lemon grass and lime
leaves (if using) in a saucepan. Bring to the boil, then cover and
simmer very gently for 10 minutes without lifting the lid. Remove
from the heat, still covered, and leave to stand for 5 minutes.
Remove the lemon grass and lime leaves (if using) before serving.
The rice will be slightly sticky.

Points per serving: 4
Total Points per recipe: 16

Whole Spice Basmati

Serves: 4

Preparation and cooking time:
15 minutes
Calories per serving: 180

Freezing: not recommended

Ⓥ

200 g (7 oz) basmati rice
1 cinnamon stick
1 bay leaf
3 whole cloves
3 whole cardamoms
2 teaspoons sea salt

This is the traditional way to cook the elegant long-grain Indian rice called basmati. Try to choose a good quality brand of basmati with few broken grains.

1. Rinse the basmati in a sieve under cold running water for at least a minute, stirring the grains with your hand. When the water passing through the sieve starts to run clear, leave to drain.
2. Meanwhile, put a large pan of water on to boil and add the spices and salt. When the water comes to a rolling boil, stir in the rice.
3. Return to the boil, stirring carefully, then lower the heat to a medium boil and cook for exactly 10 minutes from the time the water comes back to the boil.
4. Drain in a sieve and rinse under the hot tap. Set aside to stand for 5 minutes and then spoon carefully into a serving dish. Remove the spices if you like, but they do look good nestled in the rice. (Don't eat them!)

Points per serving: 2½
Total Points per recipe: 10

Tomato Foo Yung Rice

Serves: 2

Preparation time: 10 minutes
+ 15 minutes cooking
Calories per serving: 340

Freezing: not recommended

Ⓥ

A colourful version of egg-fried rice!

100 g (3½ oz) long-grain rice
¼ cucumber, sliced and cut
  into shreds
2 eggs
1 tablespoon light soy sauce
1 teaspoon sesame oil
1 teaspoon sunflower oil
2 salad onions, sliced thinly
1 teaspoon garlic purée
2 tomatoes, skinned, de-seeded
  and chopped
sea salt and freshly ground
  black pepper

1. Boil the rice according to the pack instructions. Drain, rinse in cold water and set aside. Mix gently with the cucumber.
2. Beat the eggs with the soy sauce and black pepper. Heat the two oils in a non-stick frying-pan and quickly fry the onions, garlic and tomatoes for about a minute. Season.
3. Raise the heat a little, then pour in the egg mixture and allow to set slightly. Stir gently so as not to break up the egg too much, but let the runny mixture set. You should have a mixture looking like a soft omelette but not scrambled eggs.
4. Now carefully fork through the rice and cucumber and reheat until piping hot. Check the seasoning and serve immediately.

Points per serving: 5
Total Points per recipe: 10

Chicken Biryani

Serves: 4

Preparation and cooking time:
50 minutes
Calories per serving: 445

Freezing: not recommended

Biryanis are served on feast days in India and special family occasions. This is delicious with grilled poppadums.

1 onion, chopped roughly
2 garlic cloves, chopped
2 cm (³/₄-inch) piece of fresh root ginger, chopped
1 fresh green chilli, de-seeded and chopped
1 tablespoon sunflower oil
6 boneless, skinless chicken thighs, cubed
2 tablespoons mild curry powder
150 ml (¹/₄ pint) low-fat plain yogurt
200 g (7 oz) basmati or long-grain rice
2 tablespoons sultanas
2 eggs, hard-boiled and quartered
a few sprigs of fresh coriander or parsley
freshly ground black pepper

1. Make a fresh spicy paste by puréeing the onion, garlic, ginger and chilli in a food processor. Heat the oil in a large non-stick frying-pan and then brown the chicken thighs all over. Remove from the pan.
2. Stir the fresh spice paste into the pan juices and cook for a minute. Then mix in the curry powder and ¹/₂ teaspoon salt and cook for 30 seconds.
3. Return the chicken pieces to the pan and stir in the yogurt plus 5 tablespoons of water and some freshly ground pepper. Bring to the boil and then transfer everything to a heavy-based medium-size saucepan with a well-fitting lid. Return to the boil, cover, and simmer very gently for 15 minutes.
4. Meanwhile, put a large pan of water on to boil and add 2 teaspoons of salt. When the water boils, stir in the rice and then return to the boil. Cook on a medium heat for 8 minutes, then drain in a sieve and rinse in hot water.
5. Uncover and stir around the chicken pieces. Spoon the par-cooked rice on top of the stew. Cover tightly and continue cooking for another 10 minutes. Remove from the heat, without lifting the lid and allow to stand for 5 minutes. Then gently fork the rice and chicken together.
6. Spoon on to a serving plate in a mound and scatter over the sultanas and egg quarters. Garnish with the herb sprigs and serve.

Points per serving: 6¹/₂
Total Points per recipe: 26

Mushroom and Pea Chop Suey

Serves: 2

Preparation time: 15 minutes
+ 15 minutes cooking
Calories per serving: 265

Freezing: not recommended

ⓥ with vegetable stock

Chop suey actually originated on the west coast of America and not China. It was concocted by Chinese migrant workers who built the railroads and is now popular all over the world.

100 g (3½ oz) egg noodles
2 teaspoons sunflower oil
2 salad onions, sliced thinly
1 garlic clove, crushed or
   1 teaspoon garlic purée
1 carrot, cut into long thin
   sticks
125 g (4½ oz) button
   mushrooms, quartered
100 g (3½ oz) beansprouts
4 tablespoons peas
200 ml (7 fl oz) chicken or
   vegetable stock
2 tablespoons dark soy sauce
1 teaspoon cornflour
sea salt and freshly ground
   black pepper

1. Cook the noodles according to the pack instructions. Drain and set aside.
2. Heat the oil in a non-stick wok or large frying-pan. Stir-fry the onions, garlic and carrot sticks for 2–3 minutes, then toss in the mushrooms and cook for a further minute. Stir in the beansprouts, peas and stock. Bring to the boil and mix in the noodles.
3. Stir in the soy sauce and cornflour together and then quickly mix them into the wok, stirring until glossy. Check the seasoning and serve.

Points per serving: 4½
Total Points per recipe: 9

Mange-tout Peas, Leek and Almond Stir-fried Rice

Serves: 2

Preparation time: 10 minutes
+ 15 minutes cooking
Calories per serving: 275

Freezing: not recommended

ⓥ

A simple and tasty rice dish with the crunchiness of almond flakes.

100 g (3½ oz) long-grain rice
100 g (3½ oz) mange-tout peas,
   halved diagonally
1 tablespoon flaked almonds
1 leek, sliced thinly diagonally
1 teaspoon ginger purée
1 garlic clove, crushed or
   1 teaspoon garlic purée
2 teaspoons sunflower oil
2 tablespoons light soy sauce
2 teaspoons dry sherry
   (optional)
sea salt and freshly ground
   black pepper

1. Cook the rice in plenty of boiling, lightly salted water according to the pack instructions. Add the mange-tout peas to the boiling rice for the last 4 minutes of cooking. Drain and rinse in cold water. Set aside to stand while you prepare the rest of the dish.
2. Heat a non-stick wok or frying-pan and when hot, dry-fry the almonds, stirring frequently until they start to turn golden, but do not allow them to go brown. Remove the almonds from the pan.
3. Add the leek, ginger and garlic to the pan, together with the oil, and quickly stir and toss together for about 2 minutes.
4. Mix in the soy sauce and sherry (if using). Cook for a few seconds until hot and then add the rice, mange-tout peas and almonds. Stir lightly to mix and season to taste. Cook for 1–2 minutes until piping hot and then serve.

Points per serving: 4½
Total Points per recipe: 9

Vegetables and Salads

Since many Asians have been vegetarians for generations, they have some incredibly flavourful vegetarian dishes, as you will see in this chapter. Salads are also very popular and in Thailand they are especially good. But these are not salads as we know them: hot, rapidly stir-fried foods are tossed into chilled, crisp leaves and the taste is wonderful! The recipes here can be used either as side dishes or as main courses.

Gujerati Carrot Salad

Serves: 4

Preparation time: 5 minutes
Calories per serving: 55

Freezing: not recommended

Ⓥ

Indian cooks love to serve fresh relishes with their spicy dishes.

2 tablespoons black mustard seeds or black onion seeds or poppy seeds
250 g (9 oz) carrots, grated coarsely
1 teaspoon salt
juice of 1 lemon

1. Dry-fry the spice seeds in a small, hot frying-pan without any oil for a minute or two until they start to 'pop'. Remove immediately.
2. Mix the grated carrot with the salt and lemon juice and then toss with the seeds.

Points per serving: 0
Total Points per recipe: 0

Cachumber

Serves: 4

Preparation time: 5 minutes
+ 30 minutes chilling
Calories per serving: 15

Freezing: not recommended

Ⓥ

A very refreshing relish.

½ small onion, chopped finely
4 tomatoes, chopped into small dice
4 tablespoons chopped fresh coriander
1 tablespoon fresh lemon juice
a good pinch of ground cumin
sea salt and freshly ground black pepper

1. Mix the onion and tomatoes in a bowl with the coriander, lemon juice, cumin and seasoning. Cover and chill for at least half an hour before serving.

Points per serving: 0
Total Points per recipe: 0

Cucumber and Mint Relish

Serves: 4

Preparation time: 5 minutes
+ 2 hours draining
Calories per serving: 35

Freezing: not recommended

Ⓥ

This is usually made with thick yogurt which has a high fat content. If however you drain low-fat plain yogurt, you can create the same creamy texture but with less fat.

200 ml (7 fl oz) low-fat plain
   yogurt
1 cucumber, grated coarsely
2 tablespoons chopped fresh
   mint
1 tablespoon chopped fresh dill
   or coriander or parsley
a good pinch of ground cumin
sea salt and freshly ground
   black pepper

1. Line a sieve with a piece of wet muslin or a clean household cleaning cloth (a J-cloth for example). Spoon the yogurt into the centre and leave to drain in a cool place for at least 2 hours.
2. Mix the grated cucumber with the fresh herbs and cumin. Season and stir in the drained yogurt. Don't make it too far ahead or it will thin out and become runny.

Points per serving: 1/2
Total Points per recipe: 2

Thai-style Baby Corn and Beansprouts

Serves: 4

Preparation and cooking time:
15 minutes
Calories per serving: 80

Freezing: not recommended

Ⓥ

For special occasions, use asparagus spears instead of mange-tout peas or beans.

1 tablespoon sunflower oil
150 g (5½ oz) baby corn,
   halved diagonally
100 g (3½ oz) mange-tout peas
   or whole green beans, cut
   diagonally
1 small onion or shallot, sliced
   thinly
100 g (3½ oz) beansprouts
1 fresh red chilli, de-seeded and
   chopped
1 tablespoon grated fresh root
   ginger or ginger purée
1 teaspoon light soft brown
   sugar
3 tablespoons boiling water
2 tablespoons chopped fresh
   coriander
sea salt and freshly ground
   black pepper

1. Heat the oil in a wok and stir-fry the corn, mange-tout peas or green beans, and onion or shallot for 3 minutes until softened. Add the beansprouts, chilli and ginger.
2. Dissolve the sugar in the boiling water and stir into the vegetables along with the seasoning. Reheat and cook for a minute or two, then stir in the coriander. Serve immediately.

Points per serving: 1
Total Points per recipe: 4

Mixed Chinese Vegetables in Oyster Sauce

Serves: 4

Preparation and cooking time:
15 minutes
Calories per serving: 65

Freezing: not recommended

ⓥ with vegetarian oyster-flavour sauce

Oyster sauce makes a nice change from soy sauce and is easy to buy now. A vegetarian oyster-flavour sauce is also available.

1 red pepper, de-seeded and sliced thinly
250 g (9 oz) fresh broccoli, cut into small florets
1 courgette, sliced diagonally
4 large button mushrooms, sliced
3 salad onions, sliced diagonally
1 tablespoon chopped fresh coriander
sea salt and freshly ground black pepper
For the sauce:
3 tablespoons oyster sauce
1 teaspoon sesame oil
1 teaspoon cornflour
1 teaspoon garlic purée

1. Put the pepper, broccoli and courgette into a saucepan. Season and pour over boiling water just to cover. Cover and cook for 3 minutes, then add the mushrooms and onions.
2. Cover again and cook for another 2 minutes. Drain in a colander and rinse under cold running water. This helps to keep the vegetables looking bright.
3. Mix the sauce ingredients together in a cup. Return the vegetables to the empty saucepan and reheat, then stir in the sauce. Sprinkle with coriander and serve immediately.

Points per serving: 1/2
Total Points per recipe: 2

Chinese Leaf and Sweet Pepper Salad with Honey Soy Dressing

Serves: 4

Preparation time: 10 minutes
Calories per serving: 75

Freezing: not recommended

ⓥ

Pale yellow-green Chinese leaf keeps a long time in the salad drawer of your fridge and is good hot or cold. It is particularly delicious with grilled meat or fish.

1/2 head of Chinese leaf, shredded finely
1 red pepper, de-seeded and sliced very thinly
1 bunch of watercress or a packet of rocket
1 large orange
For the dressing:
3 tablespoons light soy sauce
2 teaspoons sesame oil
1 tablespoon honey
1 teaspoon garlic purée or 1 large garlic clove, crushed
1 teaspoon ginger purée (optional)
1 tablespoon rice wine or white wine vinegar
freshly ground black pepper

1. Put the shredded Chinese leaves in a large mixing bowl, together with the red pepper strips, and watercress or rocket leaves.
2. Cut the peel from the orange; first slice off the top and bottom and then slice the peel off the sides. Make sure that no white pith is left. Cut the flesh into chunks or half moons. Add these to the bowl too.
3. Shake all the dressing ingredients together in a screw-top jar and mix into the salad. Grind fresh pepper over the top and serve.

Points per serving: 1
Total Points per recipe: 4

Spinach and Potato Balti Curry

Serves: 2

Preparation and cooking time:
15 minutes
Calories per serving: 200

Freezing: recommended

Ⓥ

Leftover potatoes and a bag of washed and prepared spinach from a supermarket make this dish very quick. To turn it into a vegetarian main course, add 200 g (7 oz) drained chick-peas.

200 g (7 oz) fresh spinach
1 tablespoon vegetable oil
2 garlic cloves, crushed or
    2 teaspoons garlic purée
1 fresh green or red chilli,
    de-seeded and chopped
1 tablespoon chopped or grated
    fresh root ginger or ginger
    purée
1 small red onion, halved and
    sliced into wedges
200 g (7 oz) cooked potato,
    cut into small cubes
1 tablespoon mild or medium
    strength curry powder
sea salt and freshly ground
    black pepper
200 g (7 oz) chick-peas, drained
    (optional)

1. Wash the spinach and drain very well, preferably in a salad spinner.
2. Heat the oil in a non-stick wok or large frying-pan. Add the garlic, chilli, ginger and onion and stir-fry for 2 minutes. Add the potato and continue cooking for another 2 minutes.
3. Stir in the curry powder and then toss in the spinach. At first, it may look as if there are too many leaves, but they soon wilt under the heat and are blended into the dish. Add a couple of tablespoons of water if you like, as the steam helps wilt the spinach. Season to taste. Add the canned chick-peas (if using). Serve hot.

Points per serving: without chick-peas 2½; with chick-peas 3½
Total Points per recipe: 5 or 7

Split Pea and Courgette Dahl

Serves: 4

Preparation and cooking time:
20 minutes
Calories per serving: 145

Freezing: recommended

Ⓥ

Dahl is an Indian word for split peas which are often made into creamy, chunky purées which are normally served as vegetable side dishes. They also make excellent light main courses if you add some other vegetables. Dahls also keep well in the fridge so why not double the quantities and make enough for two meals?

1 onion, chopped
½ green pepper, sliced thinly
1 tablespoon sunflower oil
1 teaspoon black mustard seeds
    (optional)
1 tablespoon grated fresh root
    ginger or ginger purée
1 garlic clove, crushed
2 teaspoons mild curry powder
2 tomatoes, chopped
1 courgette, chopped
425 g (15 oz) canned split
    yellow peas
1 tablespoon fresh lemon juice
sea salt and freshly ground
    black pepper

1. In a saucepan, sauté the onion and pepper in the oil for 5 minutes until softened. Add the mustard seeds, ginger, garlic and curry powder and cook for a minute.
2. Stir in the tomatoes and cook for 2 minutes or until well softened, then add the courgette and cook for another 2 minutes or so.
3. Season well and then stir in the split peas and lemon juice. Reheat and simmer for another minute or two. Serve hot.

Points per serving: 2½
Total Points per recipe: 10

Spicy Chick-peas with Browned Onions

Serves: 4

Preparation and cooking time:
20 minutes
Calories per serving: 130

Freezing: recommended

Ⓥ

Indian dishes are sometimes topped with dark brown, fried onion rings which can have a lot of Points and Calories. Here the onion slices are cooked under a hot grill to achieve the same dark colour and flavour but with less Calories.

1 onion, sliced into discs
2 teaspoons sunflower oil
2 garlic cloves, crushed
1 tablespoon mild or medium curry powder
200 g (7 oz) canned chopped tomatoes
425 g (15 oz) canned chick-peas, drained
sea salt and freshly ground black pepper

1. Preheat the grill. Lay the onion discs on a shallow baking tin and brush lightly with one teaspoon of the oil. Grill until nicely browned on both sides, turning once. Set aside and separate into rings.
2. Mix the remaining oil with the garlic and curry powder. Spoon into a saucepan and cook over a low heat for about a minute, then stir in the tomatoes. Bring to the boil, season and simmer for 5 minutes and then stir in the chick-peas and onion. Simmer for another 3 minutes and serve hot.

Points per serving: 2¹/₂
Total Points per recipe: 10

Chinese Garlic and Soy Potatoes

Serves: 4

Preparation time: 10 minutes
+ 20 minutes cooking
Calories per serving: 140

Freezing: recommended

Ⓥ

You should use freshly boiled potatoes for the best flavour and texture in this dish, although leftover potatoes will do. For a real hot zing, use a whole dried chilli crushed into flakes.

500 g (1 lb 2 oz) new potatoes, halved if large
2 teaspoons sunflower oil
3 salad onions, sliced diagonally
2 garlic cloves, crushed or 2 teaspoons garlic purée
1 large fresh red chilli, de-seeded and chopped (optional)
2 tablespoons light soy sauce
1 or 2 tablespoons chopped fresh coriander or parsley
sea salt and freshly ground black pepper

1. Boil the potatoes in salted water until tender, about 15 minutes. Drain well and leave in the colander.
2. In the same saucepan, heat the oil and fry the onions, garlic and chilli (if using) gently. Cook for about 2 minutes.
3. Toss in the cooked potatoes and mix in the soy sauce and coriander or parsley. Check the seasoning and serve hot.

Points per serving: 2
Total Points per recipe: 8

Mushrooms, Peppers and Leeks in Yellow Bean Sauce

Serves: 2

Preparation and cooking time:
20 minutes
Calories per serving: 105

Freezing: not recommended

(v)

Yellow bean sauce is made from soya beans. It comes in jars and is available from supermarkets and specialist ethnic shops. Use it like a relish to liven up a dish and add a Chinese flavour.

1 red or yellow pepper, de-seeded and sliced thinly
1 leek, sliced thinly
75 g (2³/₄ oz) mushrooms, sliced
2 teaspoons sunflower oil
1 teaspoon garlic purée
1 or 2 tablespoons yellow bean sauce
sea salt and freshly ground black pepper

1. Put the pepper slices, leek, mushrooms, oil and garlic purée into a food bag and shake well to mix.
2. Heat a non-stick wok and then toss in the vegetable mix, stirring for about 3 minutes until wilted and softened.
3. Add the yellow bean sauce and 3 tablespoons of water. Bring to the boil and then cook for another 2 minutes or so. Season and serve.

Points per serving: 1¹/₂
Total Points per recipe: 3

Spicy Tofu with Green Beans

Serves: 2

Preparation and cooking time:
20 minutes
Calories per serving: 150

Freezing: not recommended

(v)

Hoisin sauce is from northern China. It adds an aromatic, spicy sweet flavour to food. Use the diluted version for this recipe rather than the stronger and firmer hoisin paste.

low-fat cooking spray (optional)
100 g (3¹/₂ oz) smoked or marinated tofu
100 g (3¹/₂ oz) whole green beans, cut into long diagonal slices
2 teaspoons sunflower oil
2 salad onions, sliced diagonally
75 g (2³/₄ oz) mushrooms, sliced
2 tablespoons hoisin sauce
sea salt and freshly ground black pepper

1. Preheat a non-stick frying-pan which you can spray lightly with some low-fat cooking spray if you wish. When you feel a good heat rising from the pan, cook the tofu for about 2 minutes on each side until it becomes nicely browned. Remove and cut into small cubes.
2. Blanch the beans in boiling water for 2 minutes. Drain and rinse the beans under cold running water. Pat dry with kitchen paper.
3. Add the oil to the frying-pan over a medium heat. Stir-fry the onions and mushrooms for 2–3 minutes until softened and then add the tofu, green beans and hoisin sauce. Reheat and continue stirring. Check for seasoning (it may not need any) and then serve hot.

Points per serving: 1¹/₂
Total Points per recipe: 3

Indian Stuffed Eggs

Serves: 4

Preparation time: 15 minutes
+15 minutes cooking
Calories per serving: 125

Freezing: not recommended

(V)

Serve these hot or cold as a main course or starter. Delicious with warm bread.

4 large free-range eggs
1 small onion, grated or chopped very finely
1 teaspoon garlic purée
½ teaspoon black mustard seeds or poppy seeds (optional)
1 teaspoon sunflower oil
1 teaspoon mild curry powder
1 teaspoon mango chutney
a few dark green lettuce leaves, to serve
sea salt and freshly ground black pepper

1. Put the eggs in a pan of cold water. Bring to the boil and simmer for 8 minutes from the time the water starts to boil. Drain, run them under cold, running water and peel.
2. Mix the onion, garlic, black mustard or poppy seeds (if using), oil and curry powder to a paste and then heat in a small pan for about 2 minutes to cook the onion and spices.
3. Halve the eggs, scoop out the yolks, carefully preserving the egg white halves, and mash well with a fork. Beat in the onion mixture and chutney and season well. Spoon back into the egg white halves and chill until required. Serve on a small platter lined with dark lettuce leaves.

Points per serving: 2½
Total Points per recipe: 10

Sweet and Sour Vegetables

Serves: 4

Preparation and cooking time: 20 minutes
Calories per serving: 60

Freezing: recommended

(V)

Sweet and sour sauce is wonderful with this colourful mixture of vegetables.

1 celery stick, sliced thinly
1 leek, sliced thinly
2 carrots, cut into thin sticks
½ small red pepper, sliced thinly
1 courgette, halved lengthways and sliced
100 g (3½ oz) broccoli florets, trimmed small
sea salt and freshly ground black pepper
For the sauce:
2 tablespoons light soy sauce
2 tablespoons rice wine or white wine vinegar
1 tablespoon dry sherry
2 teaspoons soft brown sugar
4 tablespoons water
1 teaspoon cornflour

1. Put the celery, leek, carrots and pepper into a pan and just cover with boiling water. Bring to a boil, cover and simmer for 3 minutes and then add the courgette and broccoli. Cover and cook for another 2 minutes.
2. Meanwhile, mix together all the sauce ingredients until smooth. When the vegetables are just tender but still a little crunchy, drain well and return to the saucepan. Pour in the sauce and mix gently. Cook until everything is hot and the sauce is glossy. Check the seasoning and serve hot.

Points per serving: ½
Total Points per recipe: 2

Desserts

Don't forget desserts if you want to eat Eastern. Although almost all Asians have very sweet tooths, their delicious sweetmeats are generally not served at mealtimes, but eaten as a snack during the day. Instead after a meal fresh fruits are served, sliced and attractively arranged. Sometimes they will be sprinkled with delicate flavourings such as passion fruit juice or fragrant flower water. Always serve such platters of fruit chilled.

Mango Yogurt Mousse

Serves: 2

Preparation and cooking time: 15 minutes
Calories per serving: 85

Freezing: not recommended

It is possible to buy mangoes all year round now. They are an ideal dessert after a spicy meal.

2 teaspoons gelatine crystals
4 tablespoons orange juice
1 ripe mango
150 ml (1/4 pint) fruit-flavoured low-fat yogurt, e.g. peach and passion fruit, tropical fruit
artificial sweetener (optional)
1 egg white
chopped tropical fruits, to decorate

1. Sprinkle the gelatine crystals on to the orange juice in a small saucepan or if you have a microwave oven, in a microwave-proof bowl or jug. Stir once or twice and leave until the mixture has swelled and turned solid.
2. Dissolve the gelatine in the juice, either in the pan over the lowest possible heat, or in a microwave oven set on full power for about 30 seconds. If it needs longer, then leave it for 10 seconds or so. Leave to cool.
3. Prepare the mango. Cut either side of the long thin stone in the middle. Peel off the skin and chop the flesh. Whizz in a food processor until smooth.
4. Add the yogurt to the mixture in the processor and process again. Stir in the dissolved gelatine quickly. Tip the mixture into a bowl and taste for sweetness. If it needs any, add artificial sweetener to taste. Whisk the egg white until soft but stiff and then carefully fold the egg white into the mixture. Spoon the mixture into 2 tall sundae glasses and chill until set. Decorate with colourful chopped tropical fruits.

Points per serving: 2
Total Points per recipe: 4

Indian Pawpaw and Pineapple Platter

Serves: 2

Preparation time: 10 minutes
Calories per serving: 110

Freezing: not recommended

(V)

Serve this on a pretty dark platter or, better still, on a banana leaf – Oriental food stores often have them in their chill cabinets.

1 large ripe pawpaw
1 small pineapple or 250 g (9 oz) prepared fresh pineapple in juice
zest and juice of 1 lime
1 passion fruit (ripe when wrinkled)
artificial sweetener (optional)

1. Halve the pawpaw and scoop out the seeds. Peel the flesh and slice. Cut the top and bottom off the pineapple, then slice off the skin on the sides, removing the 'eyes' of skin with the tip of a peeler. Halve lengthways, cut out the core and slice into wedges.
2. Put the lime zest and juice into a cup and mix in the flesh of the passion fruit. (If you don't like the seeds, then rub the flesh through a tea strainer). Add sweetener to taste, if you wish.
3. Trickle this over the fruits, cover and chill until ready to eat.

Points per serving: 2 1/2
Total Points per recipe: 5

Oranges in Chinese Honey Syrup

Serves: 4

Preparation and cooking time:	4 large oranges
15 minutes + 2 hours chilling	1 tablespoon clear honey
Calories per serving: 80	3 star anise
	1 cinnamon stick
Freezing: not recommended	3 cardamom pods
	zest and juice of 1 small lemon

Ⓥ

As you'll see in this recipe, many Chinese spices, such as star anise and cinnamon, suit sweet dishes well.

1. Peel off some strips of orange peel using a swivel potato peeler. Place the orange strips in a small saucepan with the honey, 4 tablespoons of water, the star anise, cinnamon stick and cardamoms. Heat until boiling, then remove.
2. Now cut the peel and white pith from the oranges and slice the fruit into thin half moons. Save any juices from the orange and add it to the syrup as it cools.
3. Mix the lemon zest and lemon juice into the syrup. Trickle this over the oranges and cover and chill for at least 2 hours, preferably longer. Before serving, remove the whole spices and orange strips or warn diners to pick them out. Serve slightly chilled.

Points per serving: 1½
Total Points per recipe: 6

Kheer (Basmati Rice Pudding)

Serves: 4

Preparation and cooking time:	100 g (3½ oz) basmati rice
25 minutes + chilling	1 litre (1¾ pints) skimmed milk
Calories per serving: 185	1 bay leaf
	1 cinnamon stick
Freezing: not recommended	3 green cardamoms
	artificial sweetener, to taste
	3 tablespoons very low-fat plain fromage frais
	1 tablespoon rosewater (optional)
	mint leaves, to decorate (optional)
	8 strawberries, sliced, to serve

Ⓥ

Basmati rice makes a wonderful rice pudding which is delicious with fruit. You'll find rosewater in larger supermarkets or Indian food stores.

1. Put the rice, milk, bay leaf, cinnamon stick and green cardamoms into a heavy-based saucepan. Bring to the boil, stirring, and then lower to a very gentle simmer.
2. Cook uncovered, stirring occasionally until the rice becomes soft, the milk is almost reduced to nothing and the mixture becomes thick and creamy.
3. Remove, spoon into a bowl and sweeten to taste with artificial sweetener. Cool, stirring occasionally to prevent a skin forming. Chill and then remove the cinnamon stick and cardamoms.
4. Fold in the fromage frais and rosewater (if using). Decorate with mint leaves (if using) and serve with sliced strawberries.

Points per serving: 2½
Total Points per recipe: 10

Banana and Mango Yogurt Kulfi

Serves: 4

Preparation time: 15 minutes
+ 3 hours freezing
Calories per serving: 85

Freezing: recommended

Ⓥ if using free-range egg

2 ripe mangoes
2 very ripe bananas, sliced
   roughly
100 ml (3½ fl oz) low-fat
   plain yogurt
artificial sweetener
1 egg white (optional)

**This Indian ice cream has
fewer Calories because it is
made with ripe fruits and
yogurt.**

1. To prepare the mangoes, cut down either side of the long flat
stone. Peel and chop the flesh. Chop the flesh from around the
stone too.
2. Place the mango in a food processor and whizz until smooth.
Add the banana slices to the processor, puréeing until no lumps
remain. Finally, mix in the yogurt and sweetener to taste, but
make it sweeter than you usually like, since freezing will mask
the flavour.
3. Freeze the mixture. If you have an ice cream machine, follow the
manufacturer's instructions. Or pour the mixture into a shallow
plastic container and freeze until partially frozen.
4. Remove the mixture from the freezer and beat. Freeze again and
then beat. Whisk the egg white and fold in. (You will not need to
use the egg white if using an ice cream machine.) Return to the
freezer until solid. Serve Indian-style in long elegant glasses.

Points per serving: 2
Total Points per recipe: 8

Mixed Melon Salad

Serves: 4

Preparation time: 15 minutes
+ 30 minutes chilling
Calories per serving: 90

Freezing: not recommended

Ⓥ

1 small cantaloupe melon
½ Galia or honeydew melon
a nice wedge of watermelon
1 tablespoon orange flower
   water (optional)
1 teaspoon icing sugar
1 tablespoon chopped fresh
   mint

**When melons are in season,
this is a real treat.**

1. Halve the cantaloupe and Galia or honeydew melons, remove
the seeds and cut off the peel. Cut into wedges. Cut the top off the
wedge of watermelon to remove the seeds.
2. Arrange the wedges on a platter and sprinkle over the orange
flower water (if using) and icing sugar. Scatter fresh mint over the
top and chill for at least half an hour before serving.

Points per serving: with honeydew 2; with Galia 1½
Total Points per recipe: with honeydew 8; with Galia 6

Index